Becoming the Body: Embodiment Through Somatic Therapy

Exercises and Tools for Trauma, Stress, and Finding Mind-Body Connection

By Ken Michaels

Contents

INTRODUCTION

We all carry within us a lifetime of experiences, memories, and emotions, many of which have shaped who we are and how we navigate the world around us. Sometimes, these experiences weigh heavily on us, manifesting in physical and emotional pain. They can even limit our beliefs and behaviors, leading to a life lived less than satisfactorily.

But what if you could access the wisdom of your body to not only understand but also alleviate these trapped emotions? What if you could release the shackles of the past and step into a brighter, more fulfilling future? This is the vision of somatic therapy – a holistic approach that recognizes the deep connection between the mind and body and utilizes this understanding to facilitate personal growth and overcome past experiences. This book is an invitation to join me on a journey to explore and benefit from the power of somatic therapy and unlock the true potential of your mind and body.

So many of us live as though our mind and body are separate entities, yet they are both parts of what makes us whole. A disconnect between them causes deep pain. The pain of this disconnection manifests in many ways – physical pain, anxiety, depression, stress, and more. It can be as if you are living in a constant state of fight or flight, detached from the present moment and unable to find peace within yourself. It can also be like a persistent background hum of discomfort, an underlying feeling of being not quite right.

Without unity of mind and body, it is difficult to navigate the world around you, leading to struggles in building and maintaining relationships and distress at work and in pursuing your passions and dreams. Life tends to lack meaning, and purpose seems out of reach. Have you experienced this sense of feeling lost and disenchanted? Have you felt isolated and alone, even when surrounded by loved ones? Are you constantly running away from your past?

This does not have to be your reality – not anymore. From this moment onwards, you can experience the harmony that only comes with the merge of body and mind. Imagine having your every thought and emotion rooted in physical sensation and every movement and breath guided by a sense of inner knowing. Picture yourself fully engaged in the world around you and in tune with your needs and desires. In this reality, you can trust your body's wisdom and respond to life's challenges quickly and gracefully.

When your mind and body are in accord, you can respond to life's ups and downs resiliently. Even amid chaos, you can find balance. You can properly process your emotions and can manage stress and anxiety in a way that doesn't leave you feeling overwhelmed. You can feel fulfilled in your personal and professional life as you freely express yourself, build meaningful relationships, and pursue your goals and dreams.

Claim these scenarios as your future. Hold onto the image of you seeing things clearly and making wise decisions that align with your values and aspirations.

Visualize what it would be like to be content, joyful, and at peace with good health and well-being. With a united body and mind, you can live your best life, fully and completely. This image is yours to capture.

And it is entirely possible to do so by practicing somatic therapy.

Somatic therapy emphasizes the role of the body in the therapeutic process and uses techniques such as mindfulness, movement, and body awareness to address physical and emotional issues. It seeks to help individuals understand and release the physical sensations and emotions that are held captive in the body as a result of past traumas or negative experiences.

This book is your guide and companion on your journey through somatic therapy. I have gathered my many years of personal experience using somatic techniques during my own journey to bring you a workbook filled with exercises, tools, and techniques to help you learn and apply such practices in your daily life. Whether you are just starting your personal journey or are looking to deepen your understanding of somatic therapy, this book will be a great resource to help you on your path of self-discovery and growth.

To get the most out of this book, take time to fully understand the concepts and principles of somatic therapy presented in Part 1. This will give you a solid foundation for the exercises and techniques presented throughout the rest of the book. Work through the exercises and techniques in a quiet, uninterrupted environment for the best results. I recommend setting aside time in the morning when your mind is clear and free from the day's stress. This will allow you to fully engage in the exercises and be present in the current moment. Be consistent and give yourself time to adjust your mind to your new reality and balance your nervous system.

To avoid being long-winded, I say this to you finally: Welcome to your somatic therapy journey! To succeed, you need to keep a few key habits in mind. These habits will help you stay on track and avoid the common pitfalls that can impede your progress.

First, you need to have clear goals. Personal growth looks different for everyone, so you need to know what overcoming your struggles means to you. Your goals may change over time, and that's okay, but having a general sense of what you're working towards will help you measure your progress and fuel your need to keep going. Even feeling one percent better is a step in the right direction.

What is your goal?

Next, be open to the process. Overcoming your past is not a linear experience, especially as you discover aspects of yourself that you didn't know existed. Sometimes, your initial actions may work but will need altering over time as more of your past resurfaces. Keep an open mind and trust your process will work, even if the journey is not what you expected.

This book is by no means a replacement for any type of therapy or treatment. You should always consult with a licensed professional before attempting to address any serious health concerns, whether mental or physical. This book is simply meant to support you on your journey and be used as a companion. What is inevitably in charge of your journey and what is right for you is between you and your therapist or physician.

Attaining unison between body and mind does not have a finish line. Instead, it is an ongoing voyage filled with adventure and wonder. Take the first courageous step of your journey in the next chapter.

Part 1:

Starting Your Journey into Somatic Therapy

"The body is your first home. Breathing in, I arrive in my body. Breathing out, I am home." - Thich Nhat Hanh

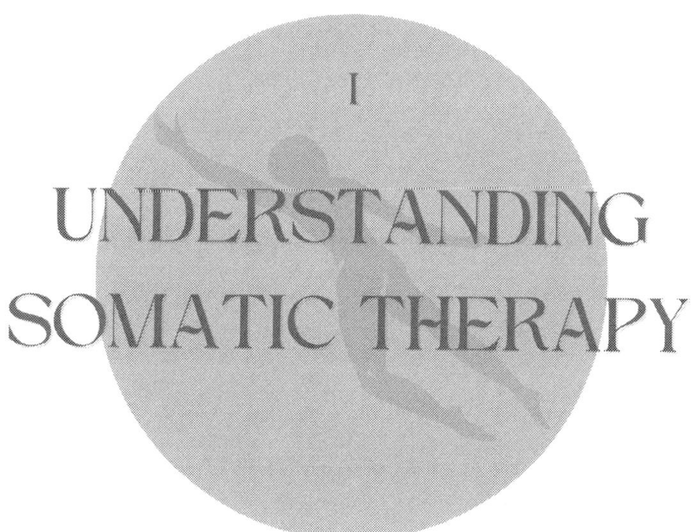

I
UNDERSTANDING SOMATIC THERAPY

Your mind and body rely on each other for optimal well-being. Somatic therapy is a holistic approach that allows you to achieve harmony between them. This chapter introduces you to what somatic therapy truly is, the techniques that will be outlined in this book, and the important vocabulary you need to know to get the most out of using these techniques.

Brief History of Somatic Therapy

Somatic practices such as yoga, meditation, and breathwork have been around for thousands of years and are often incorporated into somatic therapy sessions. However, the form of somatic therapy most practiced today is a type of somatic psychotherapy known as "Somatic Experiencing," which was discovered by Dr. Peter Levine. The term was coined in the 1970s, based on Levine's observations of wild animals recovering from traumatic events, such as being attacked by predators. Levine's observations highlighted the noticeable physical release of the animal's "fight or flight" response through trembling, shaking, or even running. The animal quickly returned to their normal state after this noticeable release. Based on these observations, Levine believes humans have the same ability to release built-up tension and trauma but often suppress or withhold these natural abilities by "staying strong" or "keeping it together" because of shame or potential judgments after a traumatic experience. This causes our bodies to become stuck in their fight or flight response, as they cannot naturally release the event and return to their normal state. The premise of his work is to help people correctly process and release traumatic experiences that have been inadequately dealt with.

A Deeper Understanding of Somatic Therapy

Somatic therapy is a body-centered approach rooted in psychology. As the term may have given away, "body-centered" refers to something focused on or around the physical body. In the context of somatic therapy, it relates to strengthening the connection between the physical body and the mind using techniques such as mindfulness, movement, touch, breathing, and grounding to help release pent-up tension and negative emotions stored in the body. This release, in turn, balances our nervous system (which we'll talk more about later). This is an altogether different approach compared to traditional talk therapy.

Talk therapy is a general term used to describe various forms of psychotherapy or counseling involving verbal communication between a therapist and a client. Talk therapy aims to help individuals understand and cope with emotional difficulties, mental health issues, and other problems by exploring their thoughts, feelings, and behaviors in a safe and supportive environment. Some of the most common forms of talk therapy include cognitive-behavioral therapy, psychoanalytic therapy, and humanistic therapy.

Somatic therapy is designed to change our state on a cellular level by addressing the negative emotions and experiences trapped within our cells. When a traumatic event occurs, the body's stress response is activated. The nervous system becomes stuck in survival mode, releasing hormones such as cortisol and adrenaline. This results in increased blood sugar, blood pressure, and a weakened immune system. Your body essentially gets "stuck" in its fight or flight response, even after the traumatic event has passed.

Being stuck in these states for long periods can result in various physical symptoms, such as chronic pain, fatigue, and immune dysfunction.

In addition to physical symptoms, traumatic experiences also lead to deeply rooted negative beliefs that are not easily accessible to our conscious minds. We are often bombarded with thoughts such as, "I am a terrible person," "I'll never amount to anything," or "I deserve all the bad things that happen to me." These negative feelings linger in the body and resurface during new stressful experiences or when experiencing triggers of our past trauma, meaning we re-live feelings of traumatization again and again.

The general premise of somatic therapy is to rekindle the connection between our mind and body, regulate our nervous system, and properly deal with and release built-up tension from past experiences.

Somatic Therapy Techniques You'll Find Throughout This Book

In the coming pages, we will review, outline, and highlight practical approaches to the following somatic therapy techniques. Within each chapter, there will be various exercises and supporting information to better your understanding of your mind-body connection journey. These techniques include:

Body awareness

This is a core component of somatic therapy. It involves becoming more aware of the sensations, feelings, and emotions that are present in your body. This is done through yoga, meditation, mindfulness, and various other exercises and prompts you will have access to. Body awareness aims to help you become more attuned to your physical sensations, identify where you hold tension, and ultimately teach you (and your nervous system) how to respond appropriately to past and present stressors. Strong body awareness allows our mind and body to work together and our nervous system to function correctly.

Grounding

In the context of somatic therapy, grounding is a term used to describe the sensation of being connected to yourself and the earth while being in the present moment, especially when you experience feelings of being overwhelmed, anxious, or dissociated. Grounding helps you feel more secure and anchored in your physical self. We will cover many grounding exercises and techniques you can use in everyday life.

Resourcing

This technique is used to help you access positive, grounding, and empowering emotions and sensations. It can involve recalling a happy memory, visualizing a safe place, or thinking of someone who makes you feel safe and loved. Resourcing aims to help you find a sense of safety and security within yourself to better cope with difficult emotions and memories. It is especially effective when partaking in somatic exercises that trigger traumatic experiences, helping you regulate your body's emotional response to keep yourself in a manageable place.

Pendulation & Titration

Pendulation is a technique used to help you process traumatic memories and emotions safely. Pendulation involves alternating between a traumatic memory and focusing on something grounding and positive, such as a resourced state. Processing the trauma in small, manageable doses means you do not become overwhelmed and can slowly adjust how your body reacts to the trauma. The technique teaches you to relax your body in a state of distress (and trains it how to do this naturally). Titration is similar to pendulation, and works in conjunction with it. The difference is that it involves gradually increasing the time spent focusing on a traumatic memory while interspersing it with grounding and resourcing. This process gradually builds your tolerance to a traumatic memory to eventually process it fully.

Self-Awareness

Self-awareness helps you see the interconnectedness of your thoughts, emotions, and physical sensations. It involves identifying patterns of thoughts, emotions, and physical sensations that happen before, during, and after a traumatic event. By understanding how your mind and body react to traumatic events, you learn to develop new, healthier ways of coping with them. You will be better equipped to deal with triggers and be able to distinguish between past and present.

Breathing and Movement

Breathing and movement are two fundamental components of emotional and physical well-being. When we engage in mindful breathing practices such as deep belly breathing, we increase our oxygen intake and initiate our relaxation response, which can reduce stress, anxiety, and inflammation in the body. Similarly, movement, through yoga, stretching, or other forms of exercise, helps to improve circulation, boost energy levels and release tension and stiffness in the muscles and joints. When we combine these two practices, we create an abundance of vitality and well-being

Benefits of Somatic Therapy

It's essential to understand what we can get out of this journey, so we're more aware of these positive changes when they inevitably arise.

The development of a positive mindset

Somatic therapy helps rewire your brain's neural pathways, moving you out of survival mode and into a conscious state of emotional balance. Negative thoughts, feelings, and patterns can hold your life hostage and keep you stuck in a self-defeatist cycle. With somatic therapy, you can finally set yourself free.

Gain self-insight

You will learn to listen to what your body is telling you, gaining insight into the thoughts, feelings, habits, and behaviors shaping your relationship with yourself and others.

Develop emotional awareness

You will become more aware of your emotions and learn to identify your body's aches and pains, which are messages from your body that you're experiencing an injury, illness, or unprocessed emotions coming to the surface.

Greater resilience

Somatic therapy gives you the tools needed to overcome recovery setbacks. The skills you will learn won't just benefit you now but will help increase resiliency for your future self to work through any challenges that come your way.

Feel freer

Somatic therapy encourages you to let go of judgmental thoughts and approach bodily sensations in a non-judgmental way. There is infinite knowledge available to you about your body when you approach learning with curiosity.

More advantages

Additional benefits that can be gained from practicing somatic therapy include:

- Reduced physical discomfort through the alleviation of physical infirmities like pain, tension, and strain in the body.
- Reduced psychological discomfort by addressing psychological distresses such as stress, negative affectivity (feelings of negative emotions), and irritability or aggression.
- Improved concentration and focus.
- Increased sense of self through self-reflection and self-awareness.
- Improved confidence. Gaining a greater sense of self and working through past traumas and negative experiences help boost confidence and self-esteem.
- Increased hope through developing a more positive outlook of the future.
- Improved relationships through improved communication gained from a better sense of self. Our reactive tendencies start to go away.
- Improved sleep quality gained by addressing physical and psychological discomfort.

- Heightened interest in activities. As a greater sense of self and well-being is gained, this proportionally increases motivation and interest in engaging in activities and life itself.

Common Terms in Somatics to Expand Your Understanding

Somatic therapy has a unique language, one that allows us to get the most out of it. Familiarizing ourselves with some of these terms will help to understand the mind-body connection and better describe what we are experiencing:

Centering

Centering is the impression of being grounded and balanced in the body. This sensation brings you back to a baseline level of awareness. Used in mindfulness practices as well as somatic therapy, centering helps you become more aware of both bodily feelings and emotional states.

Examples of centering practices include:

1. Body scanning, which is the practice of focusing on each part of your body one at a time to notice sensations and relax any areas of tension.

2. Deep breathing with repeated deep inhales and slow exhales to calm the body and mind.

3. Sensory awareness, which is the practice of paying attention to physical sensations such as the sensation of the clothes on the skin, the temperature of the room, or the sounds in the environment.

These practices and more will help you become more aware of your internal state, reduce stress and anxiety, and improve your overall well-being.

Embodiment

Embodiment is the concept of an idea, quality, or feeling being made palpable or visible in a physical form. This notion theorizes that our experiences, thoughts, and emotions are not only abstract mental states but are also represented and expressed through our bodies. After all, our physical bodies are a crucial part of our overall life experience.

For example, when you feel confident, your body posture changes. You hold your head higher and open your chest. Conversely, if you feel shy or uncertain, you are likely to hunch your shoulders and avoid eye contact with other people. In this way, your emotions and thoughts are embodied in your physical posture and movements.

Mindfulness

Mindfulness is the practice of being fully present and engaged in the current moment and paying attention to your thoughts, feelings, and sensations without judgment. This allows you to be aware of your surroundings and experiences as they unfold.

Examples of mindfulness practices include:

- Meditation.
- Mindful breathing exercises.
- Engaging in a hobby or activity with full attention and focus.

- Mindful eating or drinking, which involves giving full focus to the taste, texture, and sensation of food or drink.

- Mindful listening by paying attention to what someone else is saying without judgment or distraction.

- Mindful observation – the act of paying due consideration to the sights, sounds, and sensations of your environment without distraction.

Soma

From the Greek word for "body," this term refers to the physical body as distinct from the mind, psyche, and soul. The soma can be visualized as the material vessel that carries the self.

In somatic practices and therapies, the soma is seen as a source of valuable information about your emotional, psychological, and physical well-being. By paying attention to somatic sensations and using techniques such as mindfulness, grounding, and embodiment, you can gain insights into your body experiences and work toward greater physical and emotional balance.

Somatic psychology

Somatic psychology is a form of psychotherapy that focuses on the connection between the mind and body and how psychological experiences are stored and expressed through physical sensations and movements. Its practice helps you become more aware of the sensations in your body. This is used as a baseline to understand how these sensations are connected to your emotions, thoughts, and behaviors.

Examples of somatic psychology techniques include body-centered psychotherapy, movement therapy, breathing exercises, and yoga. In body-centered psychotherapy, the physical sensations are explored through guided movements, touch, and other physical interventions. In movement therapy, structured movements and dance are engaged to help process emotions and experiences.

Somatics

Somatics is the study or practice of the body as a whole and its connection to the mind and emotions. It encompasses any practice that uses the mind-body connection to help us better understand and listen to signals our bodies send about areas of pain, discomfort, or imbalance. Some examples of somatic practices include yoga, tai chi, and somatic therapy.

Stress response

The stress response is a physiological and psychological response that is triggered by the perception of danger or threat. This response is often referred to as the "fight or flight" response, as it prepares the body to either fight off or escape from a perceived threat.

When the stress response is activated, the brain's hypothalamus releases a corticotropin-releasing hormone (CRH). This triggers the release of adrenaline and cortisol from the adrenal glands. These two hormones are commonly referred to as stress hormones. They prepare the body to respond to a perceived threat by increasing heart rate, blood pressure, and respiration, as well as diverting blood flow from non-essential areas to the muscles. This increased physiological activity is intended to provide the body with amplified energy and strength to respond to a threat.

In addition to the physiological changes, the stress response also triggers psychological changes like increased alertness and focus and feelings of anxiety and fear. These psychological changes further help prepare you for action.

The stress response is a highly adaptive response essential for human survival against physical threats. However, when threats are psychological or imaginary, the stress response can become maladaptive and contribute to chronic stress and related health problems.

II MAXIMIZING YOUR WORKBOOK EXPERIENCE

As you've previously read, there are many different techniques in somatic therapy. This book dives deep into each, with accompanying information and exercises. They vary from simple meditation practices and journal entries to safely revisiting past events. Each section will support your learning with foundational knowledge of nervous system function and why these exercises can be beneficial. Lets get into how we can get the most out of this workbook.

Proceed at a Pace That Feels Comfortable for You

The process of somatic exercises can unearth past traumas and suppressed emotions. It's important to work through the exercises in the book at your own pace and take breaks if necessary. Remember, revisiting past trauma can be emotionally draining, so trust yourself and know when to take a break or when the supervision of a licensed therapist is necessary.

Tracking Your Progress

I am a firm believer in the power of progress. When progress is not visible, it can feel like you're stuck in a never-ending cycle. But, when improvement can be seen and tracked, it provides a sense of achievement and completion, enabling your soma to feel revitalized.

Imagine yourself as a cup filled with murky water. As you add fresh water (through self-work), the muck dissipates, and the water becomes clear, even if it's just one drop at a time. This is how I view personal transformation.

As you work through the book, take notes of the exercises you've completed and how beneficial they were (I usually like to try one at least three times before deciding whether it will work for me). As you find the tools that benefit you and you enjoy the most, list them in the table below. Rate them from 1–10 (1 being "meh" and 10 being "Felt great after") and check off how many times you've completed them. This will help you discover what works best for you and will help you build healthy habits.

Of course, every exercise has the potential to benefit you, but the key is finding essential tools we can regularly use to change our thought patterns and slowly release any built-up tension. Results won't happen overnight. Finding what works for you is most important.

FAVORITE EXERCISES

EXERCISE	RATING	TIMES COMPLETED

EXERCISE	RATING	TIMES COMPLETED

Building healthy habits are how we break away from the emotional grip trauma has held us with for so long. Changing our thought patterns and creating a new self is a crucial aspect of somatic therapy.

Pay close attention to changes in your self-awareness and perception as you progress in your journey of self-discovery. You will become more attuned to your bodily sensations and emotions and will learn to observe them before they control you. A properly functioning nervous system will also result in fewer "fight or flight" responses in everyday life and will naturally regulate your emotions.

Over time, this will enable you to move away from living with chronic stress, release pent-up emotions, and experience greater freedom in the present moment. Take note of any changes in thought patterns throughout your journey.

How to Maximize the Tools in This Book

Your first exercise starts now! Before reading, take a moment to familiarize yourself with the entire book. Skim through its contents and make a mental note of the chapter titles and exercises. Focus on bringing your awareness inward, paying attention to your breathing and any areas of tension in your body. Trust your instincts, follow your intuition, and take a brief note of any exercises that resonate with you.

The primary goal of somatic therapy is to connect with yourself and release what has been held within. I have laid out this book and its information/exercises in the most effective order for natural progression. You're welcome to trust your instincts and skip over any exercises that don't resonate with you or to continue gradually through each one. I tried to find a nice balance between useful information and activities throughout the book.

Good luck on your journey.

Part 2:

Body Awareness and Grounding Techniques

"The body is a reflection of the mind, and the mind is a reflection of the soul." - B.K.S. Iyengar

III
RECONNECTING THROUGH BODY AWARENESS

In today's fast-paced and demanding world, it can be difficult to maintain a connection with your sense of self and stay attuned to your physical sensations. When this connection is lost, it can lead to chronic pain, illness, or fatigue, as if your body is crying out for you to pay attention to it (not just on an external level, but your internal immune function as well). Mindfulness is a powerful tool to help you increase your awareness of your physical self, regain a sense of connection, and better understand your sensations in the present moment. This level of mindfulness is called mind-body awareness. This chapter will equip you with what this is, why we lose it, and what we can do to get it back.

Somatic Awareness

Mind-body awareness is the level of conscious attention you have to your physical sensations and sense of self within your body. It encompasses the perception of your bodily sensations like pain, pressure, temperature, and awareness of the position and movement of your body parts in terms of your muscles and joints. It also includes an understanding of how emotions and thoughts affect the body.

Body awareness is made possible through several body systems. The first of these is the proprioceptive system. The proprioceptive system provides the brain with information about position and movement. It helps you to maintain posture, balance, and coordination. The information is conveyed to the brain through sensory nerve endings in the muscles and joints. The proprioceptive system works in conjunction with other sensory systems, like the visual system, to give you a complete picture of your body in coordination with your surroundings. It is an unconscious process and is essential for everyday movements and activities.

The vestibular system is also involved in this type of awareness. It is a sensory system in the inner ear. It provides the body with information about spatial orientation. This is the ability to perceive and understand the position and movement of objects and oneself within an environment. The vestibular system also supplies the brain with details about your body's movement and balance.

The vestibular system is also involved in regulating the autonomic nervous system (ANS); this is a division of the nervous system that controls the body's unconscious functions, like regulating heart rate, digestion, and respiration. It helps to maintain homeostasis by responding to internal and external stimuli. It also helps control the body's responses to stress and changes in posture.

Body awareness can also be applied to sensations such as hunger, thirst, fatigue, or other bodily cues that signal a need for rest, nutrition, or attention. It can even be applied to more complex cues like physical limitations during exercises or emotional needs such as the desire for social interaction or physical intimacy.

The benefits of having optimal body awareness range from physical health to emotional well-being. By having a strong mind-body connection and being aware of your body's position and movements, you can have better balance and stability, physically and mentally. Body awareness has also been linked to weight management, pain management, improved self-awareness (mental clarity), and self-care.

So how can we lose touch when we have such insight into what is happening with our bodies?

Several factors can contribute to the loss of somatic awareness:

- Chronic stress
- Repressed emotions
- Physical trauma
- Inactivity or prolonged sitting
- Substance abuse
- Chronic illness
- Mental health issues
- Excessive external stimulation, such as social media and technology

It's exactly as it seems. Your body is constantly thinking about and experiencing an external event. What we want to do is bring ourselves back into the moment we're in and regain our mental clarity.

Starting Your Inward Journey

The path to creating somatic awareness starts as an inner journey that requires preparation. The inner journey involves exploring the inner self, which is driven by a truth-seeking spirit and is separate from the outer self, which is driven by personal illusions. In other words, you must look within. To do this, set aside quiet time often. Find a quiet and comfortable place where you won't be disturbed and can be alone with your thoughts and feelings. Be curious and question yourself. What am I feeling? What am I thinking about? Where are these feelings and thoughts? Don't be afraid to dive deep into the trenches of your mind. As you do this, focus your attention on your breath, noticing the sensation of air moving in and out of your body. Let go of any distractions and simply breathe.

You will likely notice patterns in your thoughts and feelings. This is not a time for judgment. Instead, note whether there are any recurring themes or subjects that come up. Be the observer of your mind instead of the victim.

These thoughts will stir up emotions, some you would prefer not to feel, but all emotions need to be embraced, no matter how uncomfortable. Try to understand what they're trying to tell you, and be kind and compassionate with yourself as you explore your feelings.

Looking within yourself is a journey, not a one-time affair. At no time in that journey should you rush yourself. Dealing with past experiences is not linear; there will be days when your progress is smooth sailing and others where you feel like you are at the helm of a ship in the middle of a storm. Both days are okay and should be expected, so take your time and go at a pace that feels right. Our goal is to slowly change the inner state that our body is constantly experiencing. (Remember the image of the "stuck" nervous system.)

Finding Your Baseline with a Body Scan Exercise

A body scan is a systematic and intentional mindfulness exercise that involves concentrating on each part of the body individually. A body scan aims to increase awareness of the body's sensations and cultivate a sense of relaxation and calm. The body scan helps to release tension and stress, promotes relaxation, improves sleep, reduces pain, and increases overall well-being. It is also a great place to start to increase mind-body awareness and identify where we hold emotions in the body.

How to Get Started

Find a comfortable position, either sitting or lying down. If you choose to sit, ensure your back is straight, and your chin is tucked in. Now, imagine a string pulling up the back of your head to create a neutral spine. If you opt to lie down, keep your chin slightly tucked to maintain proper posture.

During the exercise, I recommend placing your palms flat on your legs to help direct your focus inward.

What to Do (read through the entire exercise before doing)

With your eyes closed or in a relaxed gaze at something across the room, imagine a warm glow surrounding your body, almost encapsulating you. Draw your awareness to your breath. To help bring your focus inward, consider counting down from one hundred in twos, such as ninety-eight, ninety-six, ninety-four, and so on until you reach zero.

Start by focusing on your feet and toes. How do they feel? Are they tight, loose, or neutral? Neutrality, numbness, or a lack of sensation can also be a feeling. Slowly go across each toe, focusing your awareness on them. Trust yourself and your instincts as you move up your shins and slowly to your knees, feeling your joints and the muscles around them.

Allow yourself to experience any tension or discomfort without trying to force it away or ignore it. If your mind jumps around the body and you have trouble focusing, try counting down from fifty while concentrating on each body part before moving on to the next.

If you sense discomfort in your body, such as tightness in your abdomen or a pinch in your arm, give it your attention and trust your instincts. The process of exploring your inner self has no set structure; have a route in mind but be open to detours.

Keep part of your awareness on your breath. Breathe in through your belly and release any tension in your body after every exhale, allowing your shoulders to sink and jaw to soften.

Next, direct your attention to your thighs and hips, taking a moment to breathe deeply and focus on this area.

Move on to your abdomen, including the outer skin, your organs, and the base of your spine. Feel a warm glow surrounding these areas and allow any tension or discomfort to be released. Pay attention to any specific sensations or tightness you may feel in your stomach and place your awareness on these areas to help relax them. Sit with any of these parts for as long as you like while breathing slowly and deeply.

Go up to your chest and heart, envisioning the warm glow surrounding this area. Take note of any sensations or tightness you may feel in your chest or heart and consciously release them with each exhale.

Placing your awareness on a specific part of your body can be difficult. It helps to instead focus on the area around your desired focus – such as focusing on the area surrounding your heart instead of the heart itself.

Allow your focus to settle on your throat. Does it feel scratchy or tight? Ease any tension by swallowing a few times, allowing the muscles in the throat to relax and open.

Let the relaxation move into your jaw and head. Imagine a warm glow surrounding your head, both outside and inside. Concentrate on the center of the forehead, then move to the back of the head.

Let the warm sensation envelop your entire body. Observe this encapsulation from an aerial viewpoint. Notice where any tension is being held and let your focus naturally gravitate to that area. Take ten deep breaths, relaxing every part of your body.

As of now, the body scan is finished. Stay in this relaxed state for as long as you wish. Focus on different areas of the body where you feel built-up tension and work to release it, or go back down the body in the opposite order, starting with the top of your head and ending with your toes.

Tune into your body and allow it to reveal where emotions are being held.

When ready, slowly bring your awareness back to the physical world. Wiggle your toes and fingers, gently open your eyes, and take in your surroundings. Look at your hands and feet.

Follow up your body scan with a journal entry.

Why We Journal and How to Get the Most Out of It

Journaling is an effective tool for recording thoughts, feelings, and physical sensations. These records give you a deeper understanding of your inner experiences and the relationship between your thoughts, emotions, and physical sensations.

Journaling also helps identify patterns in your behavior, thoughts, and emotions. This provides valuable insights into what triggers different physical sensations and emotions and how to manage them.

In addition, journaling provides a sense of release and catharsis, allowing you to express your inner experience in a safe and supportive space. This can be especially helpful if you struggle to verbally express your thoughts and feelings. Jot down your experience however you like. Full sentences, random words, or pictures.

Journaling doesn't have to be a structured piece of writing. However, you can express how you feel.

Some key things to consider before journaling so we can get the most out of it:

1. Reflect on your experience: Writing about what you felt during the body scan reflects your experience, allowing for a better understanding. Sometimes we don't fully understand our experience of things until we organize them in an observable form.

2. Track your progress: Keeping a record of your body scans and how you felt during each one helps you track your progress and see how your awareness and mindfulness have changed over time. Note any new sensations or states of mind you experience.

3. Enhancing mindfulness: Writing about what you felt during the body scan helps you focus on the present moment and enhance your mindfulness.

Hopefully, this translates into everyday life, and you start to become more aware of your sensations throughout the day.

4. Identifying patterns: Journaling helps you identify patterns in how you hold tension and stress in your body. Over time, you can use this information to target specific areas to improve your overall well-being and find where experiences are trapped.

5. Aids in processing emotions: By reflecting on your experience and writing about your emotions and physical sensations, you process and understand your feelings better.

Overall, journaling after a body scan helps deepen your connection with your body, increase your self-awareness, and support your overall well-being.

What Did I Experience?

Now, write down how you feel. Fill out the questions and then continue to write anything that comes to mind. Some questions to ponder:

1. **Are there any parts of your body that specifically resonated with you during the exercise?**

2. **Where did you feel tightness or tension?**

3. **Is there anywhere that felt weightless or light?**

Write down any other observations in whatever form you like. Note that a lack of feeling or numbness is also worth taking note of.

By doing this exercise, you've set the stage to better understand what your body is telling you and how to vocalize it. As a result, you become more in tune with yourself. Come back to this anytime you're feeling overwhelmed, anxious, stressed, or just want a reset from a busy day.

Understanding Your Body's Sensations

The distinction between cognitive awareness and somatic awareness is crucial in understanding the holistic functioning of our being. Cognitive awareness allows us to think, plan, make meaning, and analyze. But just as important is our somatic awareness, which is not as common to be in tune with. It gives us the ability to feel and sense our emotions and instincts. This aspect of awareness protects us from stress and injury and enables us to experience joy and appreciation.

Without somatic awareness, you would be unaware of when you're tired, hungry, cold, or in danger. Valuing your sensations helps you understand how to protect yourself, when to set boundaries, and when to stop doing things that do not serve you or others well. Allowing our sensations and emotions to be processed, with the right support, can transform our state of mind and body and lead to new possibilities for experiencing life fully. This is a crucial part of our somatic journey.

While doing the exercises listed throughout this book, I encourage you to stay mindful of your emotions and the changes they go through. Pay attention to the thoughts that frequently come to mind or any bodily sensations that surface. Blank pages are provided for you to jot down any thoughts, feelings, words, or anything you want to express to aid you with this.

What Is Mind-Body Connection Actually Doing?

Sensations are the body's immediate way of telling us what it is experiencing at any given moment. But if we are internally damaged, our body isn't always right.

Our nervous system's job is to keep us safe. As such, it is always on the lookout for perceived threats, which can trigger survival instincts, even when the threat is not real or is a memory. This can result in anxiety or panic attacks, seemingly out of nowhere. We can refer to this as our sympathetic nervous system.

On the other hand, the nervous system also tells us when we feel safe or relaxed. Also referred to as our parasympathetic nervous system. Becoming aware of these cues helps us better understand our unconscious mind and, thus, minimize or have better control over these "fight or flight" events, at a conscious level but also a subconscious level, with a properly functioning nervous system that knows how to regulate our responses.

When our body senses a threat, our fear response kicks in. Sensations in this state include: **(Circle any you've experienced before)**

- Shallow, uneven breathing
- Fast heartbeat
- Muscle tension
- Hyperfocus or alertness
- Tingly arms, hands, or legs
- Perspiration
- Core tension

- Dry mouth
- Ringing in the ears
- Sudden urge to move or get out of a given situation
- The need for fresh air or an open space

When we feel safe, our relaxation response kicks in. In this state, our body can rest and repair. Sensations in this state include: (Circle any you've experienced before)

- Gurgling in the abdomen
- Yawning
- Slow and deep breathing
- Warm skin
- Relaxed muscles
- Hunger or thirst
- Flow throughout the body
- Pleasant sensations throughout the body

Both the fear response and relaxation response are crucial for our survival. Our fear response activates in response to discomfort. Your fear response, or, scientifically speaking, the sympathetic nervous system, may be active if you notice any of the symptoms above. This often results in an increase of stress hormones, blood being redirected away from the core to the extremities, efficient breathing, and tense muscles, giving us the mental focus and strength to act appropriately when needed.

On the other end, our relaxation response, or parasympathetic nervous system, helps soothe and repair the body. Together, these responses work to keep us safe and restore and repair us when necessary. Understanding what our bodies are trying to tell us in any given situation is essential.

With all of this being said, how can we optimize the function of our nervous system through mind-body connection? Let's get into that discussion right now.

Our bodies have evolved to respond to perceived threats through the fight or flight response, which prepares us to either defend ourselves or flee to safety. However, in modern society, many of us are constantly subjected to stressors such as work pressure, family conflicts, past trauma, or financial difficulties that also trigger this response. Unfortunately, these stressors tend to stick around, so the stress response is triggered on an ongoing basis. This chronic activation of the stress response is emotionally exhausting and takes a toll on our physical health as our body never gets a chance to "relax and repair."

Scientific studies show that sustained stress increases the risk of developing health issues such as high blood pressure, heart disease, anxiety, depression, and addiction. Chronic stress may also contribute to weight gain and obesity, either through direct means such as overeating or indirect ways like reducing sleep and motivation to exercise.

To mitigate the effects of chronic stress, you must engage in regular activities and practices that promote the activation of your relaxation response (parasympathetic nervous system) so that your body can rest and repair how it is intended to.

Examples of such activities are abundant throughout the book, but some common ones include meditation, yoga, mindful practices such as tai chi, and breathwork. By making time for these practices, you counteract the effects of chronic stress, ensure a properly functioning nervous system, and maintain your overall physical and mental well-being, allowing you to handle life's challenges better. Not only on our conscious level but subconsciously as well. (You wouldn't fly a plane with a malfunctioning autopilot, would you?)

Regulating our nervous system and having a healthy relaxation response comes with many advantages, such as:

- ❖ Emotional release and increased feelings of ease, belonging, and connection
- ❖ Optimal digestion and improved nutritional uptake
- ❖ Relaxed muscles
- ❖ Free, varied breathing
- ❖ Promotion of cell regeneration and an improved immune response
- ❖ Decreased pain, stress hormone levels, heart rate, and blood pressure
- ❖ Clearer thinking
- ❖ Enhanced creativity

Essentially, by connecting our mind and body, We can rebalance our nervous system so it can properly rest and repair and effectively detect threats (that are real).

Keep in mind that this process takes time and requires patience. I like to think of it as clearing a glass of muddy water. Whenever you engage in therapy, workbooks, or exercises that promote mind-body connection, it's like adding a clear water drop to the glass. With enough clear water, the mud will eventually dissipate and become clear and calm. Maybe the occasional mud will find its way in, but you're equipped with a clear glass (and many tools) to dissipate it easily.

Sensations into Words

The power of language should not be underestimated when exploring and strengthening the connection between your mind and body. Putting words to our sensations and emotions better enables us to identify and understand what our body is telling us. This, in turn, enhances your ability to tap into your relaxation response and foster a deeper mind-body connection.

Finding the right words to describe your feelings can be challenging, especially at the beginning of your somatic journey. That's why it's crucial to establish a vocabulary to use as a foundation for becoming more attuned to your daily emotions. Use these words as your groundwork and come back to them throughout the book so you can effectively describe the sensations you experience.

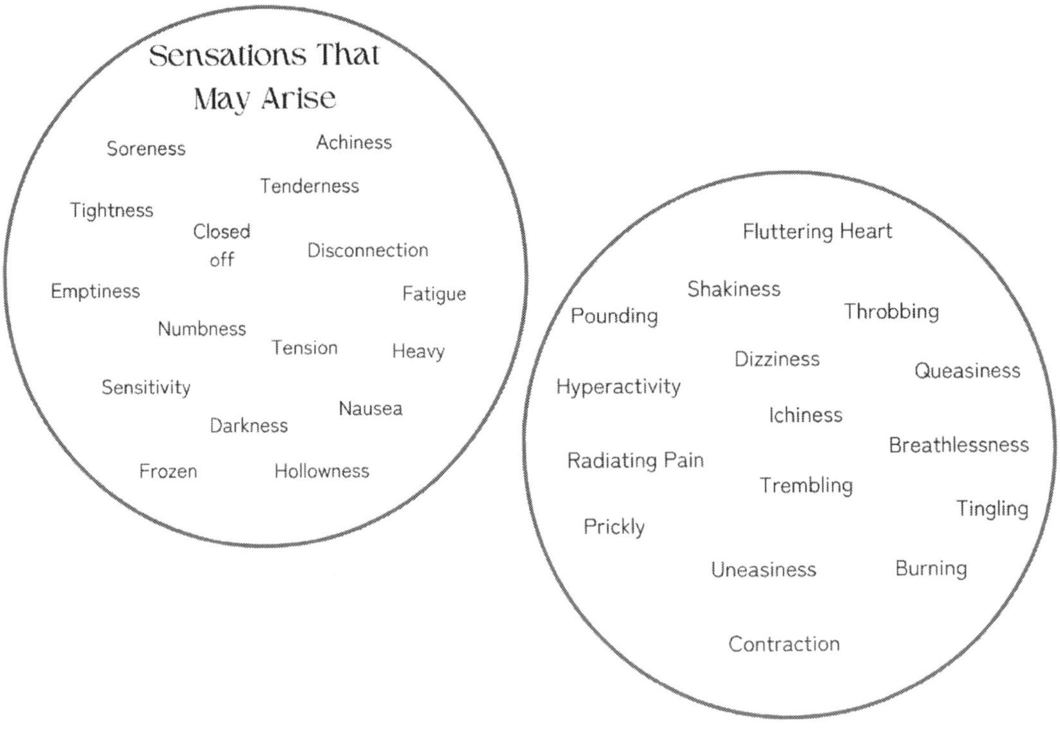

Give special attention to your positive emotions. By focusing on and recognizing these feelings, you strengthen your connection to them and avoid becoming fixated on negative emotions like fear or anxiety. If you are writing about pleasant sensations in your exercises, try using a different color pen or writing them in **Larger Letters** to showcase their value and allow them to stand out from the rest.

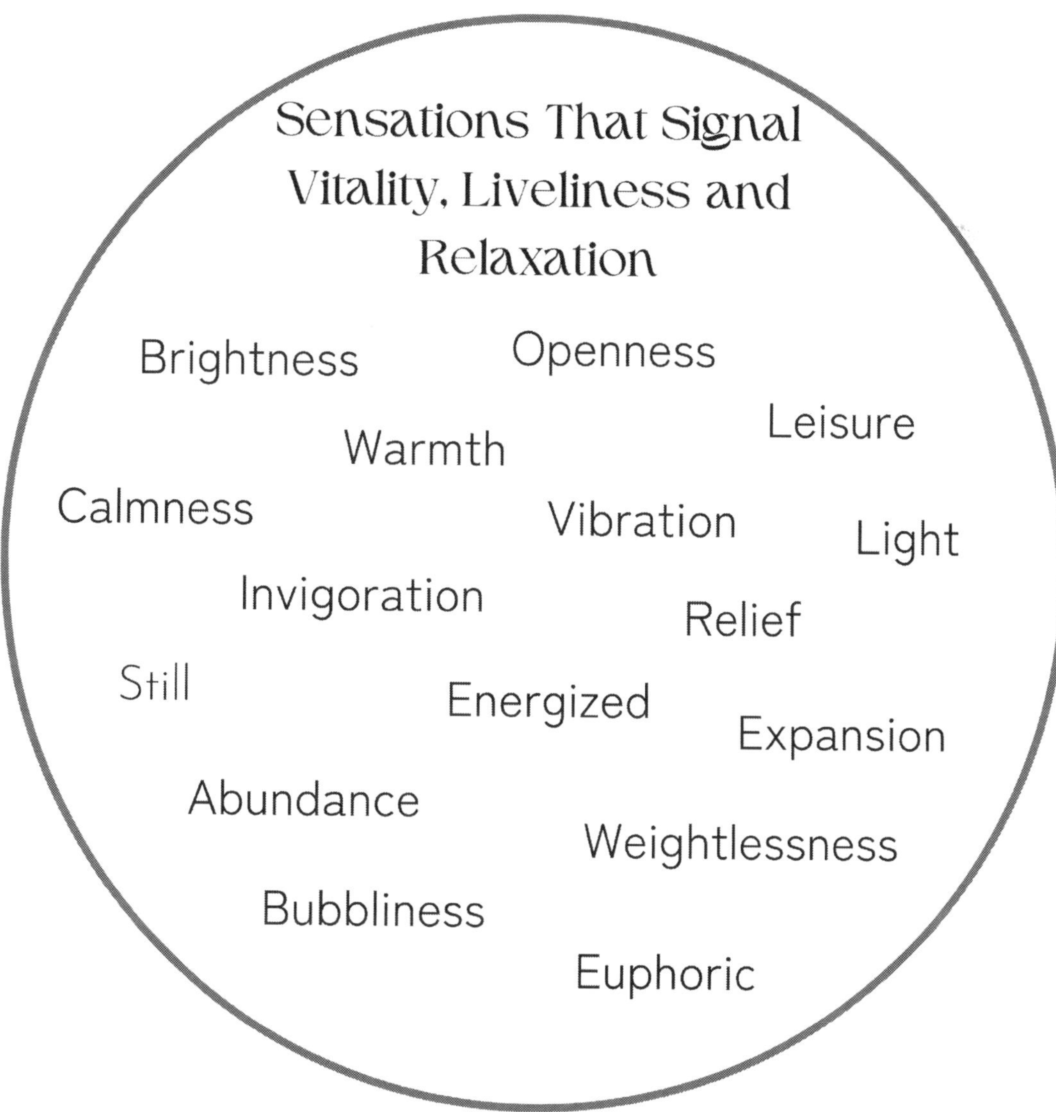

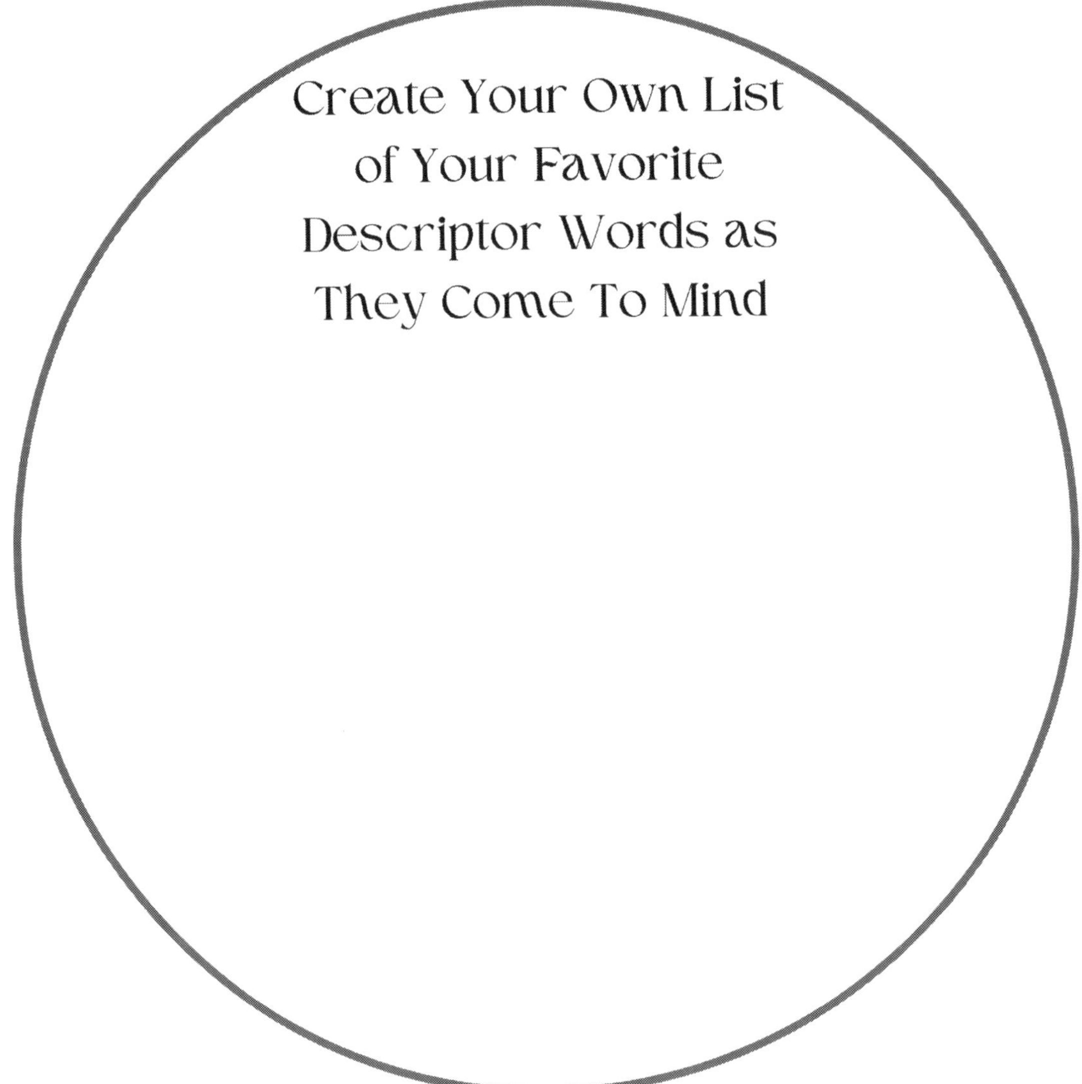

After each exercise, review these descriptive words and use them to document your experience. Practice noticing these sensations during your daily activities and keep a journal (or this book) by your bed to record perceptions at the end of the day. Observe whether certain sensations occur consistently and make a note of any emotional patterns you notice (reactive tendencies, strong emotions connected to locations, feeling safe or relaxed, or whatever else comes to mind).

Knowing more about your body helps you change your thought patterns when emotions such as anger or fear arise. By becoming aware of these emotions, you can shift your mindset to a more desirable state and catch your subconscious emotions and reactions before they take over you.

60-Second Somatic Tension Release

The following exercise is great to do regularly throughout the day to bring your awareness back to the present moment and relieve some built-up tension. It goes like this:

1. Relax your jaw and let it go slack.
2. Lower and shake out your shoulders. (We often hold tension and subconsciously keep our shoulders tight throughout the day.)
3. Shake your hands and arms out.
4. Move your eyes side to side and scan the room to notice the small details.
5. Loosen your tongue and inhale deeply.
6. Take three to four deep breaths, breathing from your belly.
7. If possible, splash cold water on your face five to ten times.

3-Minute Meditation to Bring Yourself Back

"Breathe in deeply to bring your mind home to your body."
-Thich Nhat Hanh.

Thich Nhat Hanh's words perfectly summarize how the breath is a grounding force that brings you back to who you truly are. A breathing exercise, meditation, or even a simple period of controlled boredom effectively reduces tension and anxiety. Start small to signal to your body that it's time to sit and relax.

Research shows that just thirteen minutes of daily meditation improves attention, memory, mood, and emotional regulation in those who are new to meditation. On another note, an exploratory study showed how just three minutes of mindful breathing positively affects compassion fatigue in nurses. So, start with a short meditation session and increase the length of time as desired.

What to do:

1. Take a comfortable seat, keeping your spine straight and relaxing your shoulders. Your physiology contributes to how you feel. Whether sitting on a chair or cross-legged, touching the ground with your feet can be beneficial.

2. Place your hands palm-down on your legs or create a circle with your hands on your lap. Overlap your fingers with your thumbs touching at the top.

3. Focus on your breath, feeling as each breath enters your belly and exits your mouth. If your mind wanders, return to your breath. Don't try to stop any thoughts. Be the observer of your mind, watch your thoughts, and feel your breaths. We are the sky, and our thoughts are the clouds drifting by. Sometimes, your thoughts are connected in a storm or move slowly, one by

one. Either way, we are only an observer.

4. Visualize each breath as a swing going back and forth, nothing more. Just be present.

Advanced technique: Try exhaling slowly and deeply into your belly, counting each exhale all the way to ten. If you wander off into thought, go back to one and try again. Try and make it to ten by counting your exhales without thoughts interrupting.

Aim to do this daily or two to three times a week. Just like slowly adding clear water to a dirty cup, a daily habit will yield positive results that grow and compound over time.

Enhancing Body Awareness

Take a moment to reflect on your past experiences to gain insight into your emotional patterns. This will enable you to recognize them in the moment. Mentally walk yourself from morning to night of the days that passed in the last week. With that in mind, answer the questions below:

When did I feel most relaxed throughout the week?

What sensations did I feel when I was relaxed?

Was I aware I was relaxed and embracing it, or do I only think this in hindsight?

In the coming week, focus on being mindful of relaxed moments and becoming aware of them as they occur. Tune in to your emotions and strive to understand them better throughout the day.

When did I feel stressed?

Once again, walk yourself through last week, noting the times you felt stressed.

When did I feel most stressed throughout the day?

Notice any specific points throughout the week that you felt stressed. Is there a pattern?

What sensations did I feel when I was stressed?

Was I aware that I was stressed, and was I actively attempting to change my state of mind, or do I think this only in hindsight?

When did I feel the tension or tightness? Be specific.

Where in my body did I feel tension?

What sensations did I feel when I was tense?

Was I aware that I was tense and attempting to relax, or do I think this only in hindsight?

By reflecting on your emotions and recognizing your patterns using exercises such as this, you increase your awareness in the moment and can shift toward a calming state. Regularly practicing this exercise helps you intercept negative thoughts and foster a relaxation response.

Now, an important observation to note from last week. What do I remember more of and can recall easier, the times of stress and tension or relaxation and calm?

Take note of the questions above, spend a few weeks working through the book, and come back and answer these questions again. Create a habit of reviewing these questions once a month. Have your answers changed? Are you now in a state of calm more often and can recognize it? Even if it's marginal, it's worth documenting.

Yoga for Connecting the Mind and Body

Yoga is an effective way to connect with your mind and body and experience a range of calming benefits. To get started, download my somatic yoga routine by visiting BecomingTheSoma.com or scanning the QR code below with your cell phone camera. It is beginner-friendly and designed to maximize the benefits of yoga in a short amount of time. By practicing yoga a few times a week, you can enhance the mind-body connection you seek. You can also refer to chapter seven for a visual guide to the yoga poses that accompany the downloaded routine.

NOTES

IV
BRINGING YOURSELF BACK THROUGH GROUNDING

Imagine you've had a long, tiring day at work. Your mind is racing with to-do lists and deadlines, and your body feels tight and tense from sitting in front of your computer for hours.

You step out of the office and onto the pavement and notice there is a park nearby. The sight of it immediately calls to you, and you heed the summons.

Standing in the grass, you take your shoes off, and even though the world continues to race around you, you pause and take a deep breath. You close your eyes and feel the soles of your feet connecting to the earth below you. You take a moment to wiggle your toes and feel the sensation of the ground against your skin.

As you focus on the sensation, you notice your heart rate slowing and the tightness in your muscles beginning to fade. You open your eyes and feel more present, more connected, and more in touch with your body.

This is a powerful moment, exemplifying what grounding can do for you; how it can bring you back to a place of calm and ease amidst the chaos of daily life.

Grounding places your focus on connecting and being present in your body. To do so, you must become aware of your physical sensations, thoughts, and emotions in the present moment to understand and manage them. This practice is considered an essential aspect of mind-body interventions.

Grounding techniques are plentiful. We will dive right into some that you can easily implement into your daily and weekly routines. I have put lines after each exercise so you can write your thoughts about your experience.

Physical Grounding Techniques

How to Get the Most Out of the Following Exercises

To find the exercises that work best for you, rate your condition between 1–10 both before and after you do an exercise. Rate your condition to the left of the exercise title before the exercise and to the right aftward. A rating of 1 would mean you felt bad, anything from feeling anxious, overwhelmed, or stressed, and 10 would mean you felt good, maybe calm, relaxed, or peaceful. Check whether the number increased after completing the exercise. This will allow you to see what exercises work best for you. Even if you're only one point better, that's still a positive outcome. An exercise can become more effective the more you do it.

5-4-3-2-1 Method

A popular exercise for grounding and reducing stress and anxiety is the 5-4-3-2-1 method. I find it very effective when I'm feeling overwhelmed or anxious.

To make the method even more effective, I've associated a physical gesture – like linking two fingers or making a specific hand movement – with performing the exercise. This helps my body associate the gesture with the relaxation response, and I can mentally move into that state much more quickly. (There is little scientific backing for this, but it's just something I like doing.)

When in a state of distress, anxiousness, or any time you feel like you need to bring yourself back:

List five things you can currently hear.

List four things you can currently see.

List three things you can currently touch.

List two things you can currently smell.

List one thing you can currently taste.

Focusing on the small details and immersing yourself in the present moment is a great way to bring peace and calm into your day and bring you back to the present moment. Take notice of textures and patterns, the humming of the lights (if indoors), and anything else that catches your attention. Create your own little world within the present moment. This exercise is a simple yet effective way to bring your attention to the here and now.

Feel Your Body

A quick body scan brings a manic mind back to its home.

Try and feel:

- ❖ How your legs are positioned or how your feet feel on the floor.
- ❖ The space underneath your belly button (this is referred to as your Hara and is considered your energy center).
- ❖ Whether your stomach feels full or hungry.

- The area inside your body around your heart. Is your heartbeat rapid or steady?
- Whether your arms feel loose or stiff.
- Your shirt on your shoulders.
- Whether your jaw and face are tight or loose?
- Your hair on your shoulders and your forehead.

Loosen any part of your body that feels tense once you bring awareness to it.

Use Water to Find Your Center

Water constitutes about sixty percent of an adult's body weight. It plays a crucial role in various bodily functions, including regulating body temperature, transporting nutrients, and removing waste. Water gives us life. Without it, we would shrivel up like a dry leaf.

Water is also a tool we can use to connect with ourselves. Techniques that can be used to draw on the power of water to help you feel more grounded include:

Running Your Hands Under Water

Place your hand under running warm tap water. Feel the temperature. Notice the fluidity on your skin. Now turn the setting to cold. Discern the same sensations before reverting the water temperature back to warm.

The stimulating effect of hot and cold is an effective exercise to be more present and revert your attention away from internal stressors and back to the moment we're in.

Drinking a Glass of Water

Mindfully drink a glass of water. Do not just chug it to get rid of thirst. First, take a moment to acknowledge any physical sensations of thirst and the desire to drink water. Pick up the glass. Look at it. Observe its color, shape, and weight.

Smell the water. What scent do you notice?

Take small sips to savor the taste, texture, and temperature as it travels down your throat. Pay attention to how the water feels as it moisturizes your throat. Observe it slide all the way to your stomach, lubricating on its way down.

Observe how the water affects your body and hydration levels. Once you have finished the glass, reflect on the experience and how it affected you.

Additionally, staying hydrated is important for overall physical health, which contributes to a calmer and more grounded state of mind.

Splash Cold Water on Your Face

This is my personal favorite thing to do when in need of a change of state. Splashing cold water on your face is a quick solution for calming down. This is due to the mammalian diving reflex in humans and other mammals. This reflex slows down the heart rate, redirects blood to the core to protect vital organs, and activates energy and oxygen-saving mechanisms upon immersion in cold water, preparing the body for extended underwater breath-holding.

Cold water must hit the face and enter the nostrils slightly while you hold your breath to activate the reflex. Simply submerging your feet or hands in cold water won't trigger the response. Here are the steps to get the most out of this technique:

1. Run some cold water.
2. Take a deep breath. Hold it.
3. Cup the water in your hands and splash it toward your face.
4. Repeat as desired, preferably fifteen to twenty times. (If you can't hold your breath the whole time, just hold it during the splashes.)

Take a deep breath after you are done, dry your face, and enjoy the immediate calming effects of the mammalian diving reflex.

Take a Warm, Intentional Shower

Warm water helps release muscle tension and improves circulation. Additionally, the ritual of showering is a form of self-care and creates a sense of routine, which can be grounding in and of itself. I'm sure most of you do this already. The sound and sensation of the warm water provide a sensory experience helping to focus the mind and bring awareness to the present moment. Focus on how it hits your head and flows down your body. Feel your skin absorbing and revitalizing itself with it.

In a normal shower, our mind tends to wander. Thinking about what we could've said in an earlier argument or dreaming about things we desire. Try silencing those thoughts and simply focus on your interaction with the warm water. Try and notice your state of being change, mentally and physically.

Take a Cold Shower

If you're feeling very adventurous, turn your shower cold. See how it affects your nervous system. Do you feel energized and alive? Jolt yourself back to the present. There are numerous benefits to regular cold therapy, such as speeding up metabolism, improving immune function, fighting inflammation, strengthening the nervous system, combating oxidative stress, and much more.

Proceed with this exercise cautiously. Start slowly, and gradually set the temperature colder as your body gets used to it. A sudden shock of extremely cold water can be dangerous in some circumstances.

Go For a Walk

Go for a short walk, but not like you normally do. Instead, go for a *mindful* walk, leaving behind distractions and focusing on the present moment. This is a time when you don't let your mind run rampant or focus too much on the external. Feel your steps, one by one. Maybe walk on some grass in your bare feet. Feel every blade of grass. Feel the wind blowing into your body.

Creating a mind-body connection is about being intentional with what we are doing and focusing on the present moment. Be intentional with everything you do, even if it's a simple, common task. We don't realize how beautiful living simply and being present can be until we fully immerse ourselves in it and eliminate distractions.

Extended Box Breathing

Box breathing, also known as square breathing, is a simple yet effective relaxation technique that involves deep breathing. The process consists of:

- Inhaling for four counts
- Holding the breath for four counts
- Exhaling for four counts
- Holding the breath for another four counts
- Starting the process again

The purpose of box breathing is to help calm the mind, reduce stress, and improve focus and concentration. The extended exhales help slow your breathing pattern and engage the relaxation response in your body. Try and do at least four full rotations.

Box breathing can be done anytime and anywhere, making it a convenient tool for managing stress and anxiety. I do this often. I use it when I feel anxious, before bed, before work, or whenever I need a quick reboot.

Body Tapping

Body tapping, also known as Emotional Freedom Technique (EFT), is a form of psychological acupressure. Body tapping is based on the principles of traditional Chinese medicine and the concept of energy pathways (or meridians) running throughout the body. Specific points on the body are tapped while focusing on a traumatic event or negative emotion. This technique aims to reduce stress, anxiety, and negative emotions by releasing blocked energy in the body.

Body tapping can be effective when we feel dissociated from ourselves, feel out of control, or feel numb, and it will help us return to a safe embodiment.

To do this exercise:

- ❖ Use your hands to gently tap up and down your body and limbs.
- ❖ Place your awareness on yourself and notice which areas feel more strongly than others.
- ❖ Be present and aware of the sensations.

Something To Ponder

Have you ever been lying in bed the night before a big presentation, job interview, or anything that leaves you worried, scared, intimidated, or nervous? Even seconds before, you still have shortness of breath and sweaty palms.

Write any memories of this that come to mind.

However, once the moment arrives, it's like a switch flips in your mind. Suddenly you are calm, cool, collected, and professional. Your mind and body work in harmony to handle the situation. Though sometimes nerves may take over, this is often not the case.

That's why being present is so crucial. Let's go through the same scenario but imagine going through a big event while being fully present.

You're lying in bed the night before a big event, yet all you're focused on is the warmth of your sheets and your muscles relaxing. Seconds before the big event, you focus on positive wishes or the comfort of your chair. Once in the midst of the activity, you're only focused on that. Executing, performing, and enjoying the process.

When we stay in the moment, there is no room for nervousness or anxiety, only peace. It takes time to reach this state, but the consistent practice of mind-body techniques can help. From personal experience, I can attest to the benefits of connecting the mind and body and grounding oneself. I used to struggle with anxiety, worry, and depression as a teenager, but now, as an adult, I am in control and rarely experience nervousness (all things considered, since I am still human). By consistently practicing various mind-body exercises over the past six years, I have found peace in the midst of chaos and believe that you can too.

Mental Grounding Techniques

These grounding exercises use mental distraction to take your focus away from distressing thoughts and feelings and bring it back to the present moment.

Make Yourself Laugh

When we laugh, endorphins are released to help reduce stress and create a sense of well-being. Laughing also engages the body and helps to break the cycle of negative thought patterns. Bringing joy and light into the moment leads to a greater sense of peace and stability.

Consider recalling a humor-filled moment from the past, like a colleague's silly impression, a playful moment with friends, or a fun-filled vacation with loved ones. When life gets overwhelming, sometimes the best remedy is to simply laugh and smile. Give yourself a break and watch a comedic movie that never fails to make you laugh.

Change Your Perspective for a Day

Try not to take anything seriously for a day (within reason, of course). Just feel giddy and loose. Allow weightlessness to engulf you and lift you away like a bubble. Laugh at things you normally wouldn't and welcome things you normally don't. Try to find something positive about things that normally get on your nerves. Try having a conversation with that one coworker you don't get along with. Throw all judgments aside and learn one new thing about them. Don't let that inner voice control how you think, just for a day.

Write down your experience at the end of the day and how you feel.

____

____

____

____

____

____

Leave Painful Feelings and Negative Thoughts Behind

Visualize:

- ❖ Crumpling up negative emotions and tossing them in the trash.
- ❖ Jogging away from painful experiences.
- ❖ Loading all your pent-up tension, emotions, and negative thoughts into an

airlock and launching them into the abyss of space. This one is my personal favorite.

- Simply ignore your manic mind. Pretend there is a small version of yourself in your head, talking down to you. The negative thoughts and emotions suddenly feel small when you realize they are separate from you.

Buddhists call the inner voice in our head the "Monkey Mind." This voice constantly criticizes us, but when we engage in grounding or body awareness exercises, it's like distracting the monkey. When meditating, for example, it's like making the monkey – our negative thoughts – climb up and down a tree repeatedly. Instead of directing its energy towards tormenting us, we redirect its attention and allow it to focus on other things. Eventually, it will leave us alone. The more we practice these exercises, the better the monkey becomes at entertaining itself and not bothering us.

Memory Game

I often play this little game when traveling with friends, on a road trip, or when I need to entertain my monkey mind.

1. Pick a category. Movies, songs, places, musicians, vegetables, whatever you like.

2. Now start with A, and try and think of a movie (in this case) that starts with A. Then do the same with B and C, and so on.

Soothing Grounding Techniques

Soothing techniques are meant to comfort you when you're feeling emotionally distressed, anxious, overwhelmed, or whenever you feel you might need them. Promoting good feelings can help the negative feelings fade.

Practice Self-Kindness

Positive affirmations are short and personal statements that you repeat to yourself to promote positive thinking, boost self-esteem, and overcome limiting beliefs and negative self-talk. Focusing on positive statements that promote self-love, confidence, and positivity shifts our perspective and creates a more calming and stable mental state, especially when done regularly.

Positive affirmations can be used as a grounding tool because they help to reframe negative thoughts and bring attention to the present moment. Examples that you can repeat to yourself include:

"These emotions do not define me. They will pass like they always do."
"I am strong. I can endure any pain and overcome it."
"I am giving my best effort, and that's all that matters."

Come up with your own words that make you feel good.

Breathe deeply, and speak them with intention. Our thoughts become who we are. What we tell ourselves daily drastically impacts how we feel and who we become, especially over time. Get creative with your affirmations and tell yourself what you need to hear, given the situation.

Try coming up with affirmations daily, possibly every morning, to start the day off right. Healthy habits like this are a way to slowly remove any intrusive thoughts from our brains and change the way we think about ourselves and our experiences.

Write down some affirmations you want to tell yourself.

Visualize a Time When You Felt Your Best Self

Maybe a time, a place, or a year. Visualize when you truly felt like the real you. Go deep with this. Remember that this person is still you, even if they haven't been around for a while. If you've felt it before, you can feel it again. Identify with this feeling. Write down what you come up with.

Picture Someone You Love

Picture the voice and face of someone you love or someone positive in your life. Imagine them. How do they make you feel?

Additional Tips

Grounding yourself isn't a magical experience that will instantly relieve all your problems. It is likely to be challenging. The best way to stick to it is to find the exercises you like best and do them routinely when you need them so your body can associate the exercises with calmness and safety. Over time, they will work better and better.

Some tips to get the most out of the exercises include:

Avoiding Judgment

If, for example, you're picturing a place or scanning your environment, focus more on the thing itself instead of how you feel about it. Don't let yourself judge the environment you're in. Just observe it. What we think is bad or good isn't always accurate when in a state of distress.

Practicing consistently

Practice these techniques frequently. Do them even when you don't need them. If you make these exercises feel normal and easy during normal happenings[CB11] , they will be easier to fall back on when anxious or distressed because you won't be trying to learn a new process. I like to do at least one grounding exercise per day.

NOTES

Part 3:
Emotional Regulation

"The body is the physical manifestation of the mind." - Deepak Chopra

V
CENTERING YOURSELF THROUGH RESOURCING

Did you know that over eighty percent of the body's sensory receptors are located in the skin and muscles, making them crucial for regulating your emotions and stress levels? This is the basis of somatic resourcing, a technique that utilizes your body's sensory input to regulate emotions, thoughts, and behavior.

The word "somatic" comes from the Greek word "sōma," meaning "body." In this context, "somatic" refers to the physical sensations and experiences of the body. The word "resourcing" refers to the act of using something to support or replenish oneself, in this case, using the body's sensations to regulate emotions and stress. Together, "somatic resourcing" means using the body's sensations to support and improve overall well-being.

Somatic resourcing is rooted in the fields of psychology and somatic therapy. It has evolved from various approaches, including body psychotherapy, the Hakomi Method, and Sensorimotor Psychotherapy. Hakomi is a mindfulness-based psychotherapeutic approach focusing on the present moment experience and unconscious patterns to facilitate psychological growth. Sensorimotor Psychotherapy is a body-oriented therapy that utilizes physical sensations and movements to process and deal with trauma stored in the body.

The concept of somatic resourcing was popularized in the 1970s and 1980s with the growing popularity of mindfulness and the integration of Eastern philosophy into Western psychology. The practice draws from multiple disciplines, such as anatomy, physiology, psychology, and mindfulness, to provide a holistic approach to regulating emotions and stress.

This chapter will give you the information you need to effectively utilize this somatic therapy principle.

What Is Somatic Resourcing For?

Somatic resourcing is a tool used for various purposes, including in cases where somatic exercises make you re-live potentially triggering memories or when facing triggers in daily life that may evoke traumatic emotions. This approach provides a foundation of calmness and stability that can be accessed and relied upon in difficult moments. It is important to remember the resources you have available to you and to continue utilizing them throughout your journey of self-exploration and growth.

Before You Begin

Discover the power of your internal resources with the prompts listed on the following pages. These prompts are designed to help you access the power that already exists within you. We are not trying to create new resources. Rather, it is important to tap into what is already available to you and what your body naturally knows is a safe place.

For maximum benefit, approach this exercise when you are in a stable state of mind and body. Avoid times when you feel particularly triggered, hungry, tired, distracted, irritated, or hyper. To create a positive and productive experience, locate a quiet and reflective space where you can be alone, still, and relaxed.

Once there, adopt a comfortable seated position in a chair with an upright and relaxed spine and unobstructed breathing. Position yourself so that your feet are flat on the ground. This will help to create an environment of calm and focus, so you can fully connect with your internal resources.

How to Effectively Discover Your Somatic Resources

Answer the questions below to find your somatic resources. Feel free to skip any prompt if it is too challenging or emotionally difficult. You can always go back to it later when you think you have better resources to handle the load.

Tune in with yourself to notice any sensations or emotions throughout your body, even if they are subtle. Take note of neutral or pleasant emotions or any contradictory emotions, such as if you feel simultaneously happy and sad.

Try to sit with each prompt to the best of your ability. Try closing your eyes to really pull something from it. Closing your eyes helps to:

- Better visualize the scene
- Better feel/notice physical sensations
- Reduce any outside stimulants

Below is a list of vocabulary you can reference if you are having trouble finding the words.

Peaceful	Still	Airy
Satisfied	Vibrating	Sparkling
Content	Connected	Expansive
Fulfilled	Full	Flowing
Patient	Brimming	Breezy
Present	Glowing	Fluid
Serene	Cozy	Light
Trusting	Buzzing	Awake
Compassionate	Pulsing	Supported
Excited	Radiant	
Proud	Settled	
Joyful	Bubbly	
Amused	Quiet	
Ecstatic	Centered	
Relieved	Grounded	
Calm	Gentle	
Loving	Warm	
Happy	Cool	
Open	Energized	
Effortless	Spacious	

Things You Love

Thinking about your favorite things is an easy way to center yourself and remind yourself of all the joys in your life.

Let yourself feel as much as you can. Fill in each category below with things you love that make you feel calm.

Scent

Favorite foods or experiences you've had with food

Sounds or songs (for me, music is my ultimate anti-depressant)

A season or time of year and why?

A place to curl up where you feel safe

Activity or sport

Exercises, stretches, or any type of movement that makes you feel good

Parts of your body you love

A compliment you've received that warmed your heart

Prompts

Fill out the prompts below. Write any extra thoughts or feelings you have about each prompt. If you can't quite remember, that's fine too. Make a note of it.

1. ***What is your fondest memory? How did you feel at that moment?***

The memory:

Sensations you experienced in your body:

The emotions you felt:

Where you felt them:

Extra comments:

2. *What is the most beautiful place you've visited? Imagine revisiting this place. You can see the entire view around you and can feel the temperature. Imagine how it feels to be there. Place yourself there and remember all the small details.*

The place:

Sensations you experienced in your body:

The emotions you felt:

Where you felt them:

Extra comments:

3. *Who is someone you cherish? Picture them with you, smiling.*

Who are they?

What makes them so special?

Sensations you experienced in your body when interacting with or remembering them:

The emotions you felt:

Where you felt them:

Extra comments:

4. *What is something you cherish? This could be an object, a pet, a hobby, or something you couldn't live without.*

What is it?

What makes it so special?

Sensations you experienced in your body interacting with or remembering them:

The emotions you felt:

Where you felt them:

Extra comments:

5. *Where is your safe place? This could be someone else's house, a vacation spot, a part of your home, or a place in your city. Think of a space where you're always welcome and feel safe.*

Where is it?

What makes it so special?

Sensations you experienced in your body when there:

The emotions you felt:

Where you felt them:

Extra comments:

6. For the final question, simply write anything that truly makes you happy, the first thing that comes to mind when thinking about something that makes you feel alive or at peace. This could be anything. Either something you've written down already or something that has been in the back of your mind for a long time. It could be a dream vacation or a dream lifestyle. Elaborate as much or as little as you like.

Identifying Your Resources

Go through the exercises and prompts you just filled out. Sit with them again and feel how they affect you. Take your time. Now, circle anything that gives you strong body sensations and the most pleasant emotions.

Do this a second time, slowly going through them again. Circle any of them that didn't give you any unpleasant emotions or negative sensations. Don't worry about circling some of these twice.

Whichever ones have been circled twice can confidently be used as your resources. It's okay to have a few different ones so you have many safe places to go.

How to Use Your Resources

Resources are to be used when you are in an uncomfortable place. This discomfort can be initiated by anxiety, triggers, reliving traumatic memories in other somatic exercises throughout this book, or any time you feel physically or emotionally overwhelmed.

Whenever I use somatic resourcing, I close my eyes, take a few deep breaths, count back from ten while breathing deeply, and imagine myself experiencing my chosen resource.

You can also have a physical prompt, such as clenching your hand, placing two fingers together, or anything else that is relevant. This action prompts you to reach for your resource. Over time, you'll get accustomed to associating this action with your safe places, and it will become a reflex.

Actively revisit your resources every day, even if you have no reason to. This will make them easy to visit when you're overwhelmed and will allow your body to spend more time in a relaxation response to train it to transition more easily.

Other Resources You Can Use in Everyday Life

When feeling anxious or overwhelmed, these are a few things I like to partake in or use as a resource when I need a reset.

Get Some Fresh Air and Exercise

Fresh air and exercise are a powerful combo for encouraging connection with your resources. I personally love to get outdoors for a deeper grounding experience when I feel like life is too much. Go for a run or a walk. Feel the fresh air on your skin and in your lungs. Feel yourself on the ground of the earth. Let your mind be still. Put your bare feet on the ground or in some water. All of it and more compound into a distinct stabilizing experience. Be intentional with something as simple as a walk and try and be as present as you can.

Breathing grounds you by shifting your focus to the present moment and calming your nervous system. Controlled and slow breathing reduces the heart rate, decreases anxiety, and brings a sense of peace and calm to the body and mind. In essence, it deactivates the stress response and flips the relaxation switch on.

By paying attention to the sensations of breathing – such as the movement of the diaphragm, the sensation of air entering and leaving the nose or mouth, and the rise and fall of the chest – you anchor yourself in the present moment and reduce stress and anxiety. And what better place to be when you find the anchor than in nature, a place that feeds serenity into your lungs? Additionally, deep breathing increases the amount of oxygen in the body, improving focus and clarity of thought.

Engaging in physical movement like walking in the park or even swinging your feet as you sit beside a lake initiates the release of endorphins, which reduce stress, anxiety, and depression. Additionally, being active outside or in nature enhances your grounding experience as you can take in the sights and sounds of your surroundings.

Take Time Alone

Time spent alone is seen as a largely taboo thing to do in a culture where everyone is always connected. However, intentional, mindful solitude is needed to clear the mind, refocus, and recharge your body. Think of time alone as a tool that centers you and gives you clarity. It takes away distractions, so you have a clearer vision as you reconnect with who you are and create a vision of who you want to become. This is a resource that anyone and everyone can harness the power of.

Suggestions for deliberately using time alone as a somatic resource include:

- Giving yourself a hug
- Doing yoga
- Meditating
- Engaging in breathing practices
- Journaling
- Taking a warm bath

- Snuggling up in a comfy blanket and watching a good movie

What to Do When You're at Work

The workplace is typically overwhelming, and you likely feel you can't fully relax until you get home. As such, work is a space that normally requires the use of resourcing. A few activities you can do in such a setting (or any other that introduces anxiety, fear, or stress into your day) include:

- Feeling a string pulling the back of your head to recenter yourself and straighten your posture.
- Focusing on slow, deep, belly breathing
- Feeling your feet on the ground
- Complimenting a coworker to introduce positivity into the atmosphere
- Trying to have your lunch outside or somewhere new
- Splashing cold water on your face

Forest Bathing

"Forest bathing" or "taking in the forest atmosphere," also known as shinrin-yoku, is the Japanese concept of spending time in nature to improve health and well-being. Health benefits of forest bathing include reduced stress and anxiety, improved mood, lower blood pressure, boosted immune system, and increased feelings of calm and relaxation. Believe it or not, in Japan, some companies request a mandatory time frame per week you must spend in nature to experience these calming benefits.

To practice forest bathing, aim to immerse yourself in nature and engage all of your senses. Feel the plants, smell the forest aromas, and listen to birds chirping and leaves rustling. Taste the fresh air. Practice mindfulness and focus on the present moment. Look for moments of wonder and appreciate the beauty of nature around you, whether it's a beautiful sunset, a crystal-clear stream, or the changing of the leaves.

I implore you to use the resources you have discovered for support if the memories become too intense or you feel overwhelmed while doing the exercises in this book.

NOTES

VI REBALANCING THROUGH PENDULATION & TITRATION

Before we delve into this chapter, I must emphasize something important. Pendulation exercises can allow you to reflect on past events that may have been traumatic or emotionally charged. However, revisiting traumatic experiences can be challenging and may evoke strong emotions, which can be triggering despite the potential benefits of facing them.

It is crucial to take things at your own pace and avoid revisiting anything too overwhelming immediately. If you find revisiting these events too difficult, only do so once you are in the presence of a licensed therapist who can provide support and guidance. With that being said, let's explore what pendulation is and how it can help you.

Understanding Pendulation

Have you ever found yourself caught in the grips of past stress or anxiety, unable to break free from the cycle of negative thoughts and emotions? You can bring yourself out of that loop using pendulation. The process shifts your focus between stressful content and something that evokes a relaxation response. This technique is sometimes referred to as looping because of the continuous alternation between conflicting states and trauma-related states.

For a healthy individual, the nervous system is in a state of continuous expansion and contraction, with periods of stress and calm alternating throughout the day. This natural process helps the body respond effectively to different situations and cope with stress. During periods of stress, the nervous system activates the body's fight or flight response, preparing it for action. During periods of calm, the nervous system returns to a state of relaxation, allowing the body to rest and recover. However, when we are exposed to repeated traumatic experiences, our nervous system becomes stuck in a state of high arousal (contraction), leading to symptoms of anxiety, depression, and other related disorders.

Think of pendulation as a soothing back-and-forth motion, where we loop between conflict-free states and trauma states. By intentionally shifting our attention between these two states, we allow our nervous system to regulate and find a more balanced, calm state when experiencing a fight or flight response. The alternation between traumatic content and a calming or safe memory allows the body to transition from a state of contraction to a state of expansion, reintroducing the natural rhythm of expansion and contraction disrupted by trauma and reintroducing the ability to regulate itself on its own.

How Does Titration Come into Play?

Trauma and its accompanying emotions, like panic, fear, terror, anger, frustration, and depression, often manifest as physical sensations in the body, like feeling overheated, trapped, frozen, disconnected, or lost. When addressing these emotions and experiences, it is important to approach them in a body-centered manner and at a pace that allows the body to tolerate discomfort and release the emotions effectively. This is achieved through the use of titration and pendulation in conjunction.

Titration involves processing small amounts of stress or discomfort at a time to release and discharge tension from the body. This approach helps regulate the nervous system and promotes a sense of control, allowing for the effective processing and release of emotions during challenging times.

In chemistry and medicine, titration refers to the process of determining the quantity of a substance in a solution by adding a measured amount of a second substance of known concentration until a reaction is complete. This reaction is usually indicated by a change in color or a specific observable endpoint. The point at which the reaction is complete is known as the equivalence point. The quantity of the first substance can be calculated based on the amount of the second substance used.

The process is widely used in analytical chemistry, quality control, and clinical laboratory applications to measure the concentration of various chemicals, including acids, bases, and electrolytes. In medicine, titration is often used to adjust the dose of medication to the appropriate level for a patient based on their age, weight, and other factors.

Titration is a concept not limited to chemistry or medicine. It is also applied to human functioning. In the field of somatic psychology, the term "titrate" is used to describe the level of emotional flow we allow into our internal system. When an individual experiences too much trauma too quickly, the body can become overwhelmed and lose its ability to process, integrate, and manage emotions.

To titrate the experience, individuals start by slowly exposing themselves to past traumas (hence why it is also called slowing or portioning) and then retreating to a state of relaxation. The process begins with lighter experiences and gradually works its way up to larger, more traumatic events. The idea behind titration is to maintain control and safety over our emotions by regulating the amount that we allow into our system through gradual exposure. With practice, titration can be mastered and used as an effective tool for emotional regulation.

Creating a Foundation

Pendulation is a helpful exercise for strengthening your connection with the different parts of your inner universe, whether they feel lost or found, fragmented or whole. Living with trauma is difficult, especially if you feel constantly triggered and on edge. Small things like a sound or a smell can set off a chain reaction of fear and anxiety that leaves you feeling lost and shattered. This causes problems with decision-making and makes it arduous to focus and handle daily life.

But with pendulation, you can learn to regularly shift your focus to something completely unrelated and calming. This lesson starts with developing a better relationship with your unresourced and resourced parts of consciousness.

The concept of "resources" is also central to somatic exercises. A quick recap: A resource is any internal or external factor that can help you feel more grounded, safe, or regulated when in a time of stress.

These might include memories of positive experiences, physical sensations of comfort or support, or other forms of support or connection. For example, you might identify a memory of a time when you felt loved and supported and use that memory as a resource to help you feel more grounded and connected in the present moment. Or, you might use a physical sensation, such as the feeling of your feet on the ground, to feel more present and embodied.

On the other hand, the "unresourced" parts of you are those aspects that feel scared, hurt, or overwhelmed and don't have the tools or support needed. These parts of you tend to feel lost and disconnected and require resources to help you feel safe, calm, and whole again.

Ultimately, accessing these resources aims to help you develop a more empowered and conscious relationship with your own experiences to live more fully and freely in the present moment.

Luckily, you should have already discovered the resources available to you by doing the exercises in chapter 5. If you haven't already, please refer back to that location to find your resources.

Understanding Your Resources for Effective Results

Visiting your resources before engaging in a pendulation exercise is essential to getting the most out of it. Understanding what we are supposed to feel when in a resourced state creates a safe space we can quickly get to and know we can rely on. Over time, you will master the art of relaxing your nervous system, but it's essential to get an initial baseline, so we understand what exactly our resources are doing for us. You can try visiting a few of your resources if you have more than one and move forward with the most effective one.

One way to strengthen your resources is to find a calm place in the body to pair them with. By going to our resources, while focusing our awareness on a safe part of our body, we can more effectively take ourselves out of a triggered state and into a relaxed one. You can find your safe space by following the exercise below.

First, get comfortable lying or sitting, then take yourself to your chosen resource. While thinking about this place, take a moment to scan your body and find anywhere that feels settled, supported, grounded, connected, satisfied, comfortable, or content. Spend some time exploring your body with your awareness to find this place. When found, explore this area. Find where the warmth is strongest. Even if the sense of calm is subtle or fleeting, just observe it and notice how it feels. Use words like calm, relaxed, peaceful, or content to describe it, or experiment with giving it a name that resonates with you.

Build on this by exploring your body for a different kind of sensation. A deeper one that you have yet to pay much attention to. It's a space of calm and tranquility, a place of natural ease and peacefulness that can help you find balance and stability. When visiting your resource, this place in your body may light up with warmth and tingles. Call this spot your safe place. Your hands could be your safe place if your resource is you throwing clay on a pottery wheel. Combining your visualized state with a part of your body will fully submerge and enhance you in your resource.

Remember that you can draw upon many types of resources, including imaginary places, people, or beings, and memories of peaceful moments – anything that brings you to a state of relaxation.

Write down your most effective resource and safe space.

Mapping Out Your Traumatic Experiences To Revisit

Before you begin, fill out the chart below with memories you want to revisit and work through. Write down any traumatic experiences in the chart, but please proceed with caution and do not revisit anything too intense if you do not feel ready. Start doing your pendulation exercises with mild experiences and work your way up to tougher memories.

Scale to use: 1-10, with 1 representing mild trauma and 10 representing extremely traumatic experiences.

Begin with recalling more mild experiences (rated from 1-4), then gradually move up to more traumatic experiences that you wish to overcome (rated from 6-10). It is okay to include experiences that fall in between these ratings as well.

EVENTS TO REVISIT		OBSERVATIONS AFTER EXERCISE	
EVENT (SINGULAR OR RECURRING	RATING	SENSATIONS WHEN REVISITING	RATING AFTER EXERCISE
Getting lost in a public place as a child and feeling scared	3	Frozen. Fast heartbeat, Trembling, Scared	2 less triggering after 3 sessions. Sensations not as strong

EVENT	RATING	SENSATIONS WHEN REVISITING	RATING AFTER EXERCISE

Pendulation Exercise

Before you start, please note that you should take caution not to go too deep too fast. Start by picking one trauma from the chart and gradually work your way down the list over time. Eventually, you can work up to revisiting extremely traumatic events.

The steps:

1. Find a comfortable spot and lay down, or sit with your hands on your thighs.

2. Begin by revisiting the trauma you have chosen from the chart. Focus on your body and the sensations that arise. Utilize vocabulary you've acquired throughout this book to convey emotions accurately. If the feeling is particularly intense, you can focus on the periphery of it, like selecting a single tennis ball from a pile or picking a single apple from a tree. Remember, if you feel overwhelmed, take only one. Possible emotions or states you may experience could be your physical body (such as tension or pain), your emotional body (such as sadness or regret), or your energy fields (such as pulsation or tingling). It's okay to focus on only one subtle sensation the first time.

3. Next, go to your resource or "safe place." Transport yourself to a place of relaxation and calm and let it fully embrace your body. Keep imagining this place until you feel it calming you down.

4. When you feel relaxed and calm, slowly move back and forth between the trauma and the safe place, paying attention to what happens. Take note of any release of tension or discharge of trauma, such as shakes, deep breaths, temperature changes, tears, or easier breathing. This is normal. Through this process, your body regains its ability to self-regulate.

5. Finish with a relaxing place. Let your body naturally calm down before finishing. Try staying still and breathing for a bit longer after you finish. Note whether you're calmer than when you started, even if just slightly.

Please note that you should not attempt to revisit extremely traumatic events without the presence of a therapist. When you're ready, you can revisit very traumatic events and use various actions to release tension under the supervision of a professional.

Congratulations! You have just learned to self-regulate from a state of activation on your own.

You can use this process as much or as little as you like to slowly learn to bring yourself out of fight or flight and back to a relaxation response, progressively working with more traumatic memories.

NOTES

Part 4:

Creating Awareness for Long Term Relief

"The body is a living temple. Honor it, enjoy your life, and nourish it with awareness." - Maria Villella

Why You're Reading This Book

In my early 20s, I was facing a challenging phase in my life and was struggling to figure out the direction needed in order to undergo a much-needed personal transformation. I stumbled upon a book about mindfulness and although I was never much of a reader or one to get into self-help books, this time was different. I had found myself in the "reviews" section and there was a personal story from a reader that resonated with me deeply. Their story started out exactly where I currently was and ended exactly where I wanted to be.

Reading that review was the catalyst that not only led me to obtain the book but also sparked my own personal journey toward growth and transformation. This journey ultimately led me to where I am today and is the reason why you are reading this book.

I will always be grateful to that book reviewer for sharing their story and for inspiring me to take that first step.

You have the power to provide guidance and encouragement to someone who may be struggling to overcome their own challenges. Your words could be the catalyst that helps them take their first step towards transformation, offering a sense of hope and possibility to those who may be feeling lost and alone. Don't underestimate the impact of your voice in helping others find their way toward a brighter future.

For a bonus exercise in this book, I would like to invite you to take a moment and share your honest thoughts on Amazon. By sharing your experience, not just with this book, but with your own journey, you can inevitably help someone start a new journey and find the motivation to push through and overcome their challenges.

By writing down a brief account of your personal journey, you can gain a broader perspective on the progress you have made and the obstacles you've pushed through, even when it feels like you've made no progress at all.

You can return to your review monthly and see how many people you've helped. Prospective readers have the ability to mark a review as helpful, which is indicated below your review.

8 people found this helpful

Helpful | Report abuse

You can share your honest thoughts on "Becoming the Body" at Review. becomingthesoma.com. Or on your amazon orders page.

Always remember that you are not alone on your journey.

VII RELEASING THROUGH SELF-AWARENESS

Trauma is a curious beast. It is something that can happen to anyone, anytime, anywhere. The idea that trauma only happens to certain people is a misconception that has been perpetuated for far too long. It is a myth that has been used to create a false sense of security for those who believe they are immune to its effects. But the truth is: Trauma does not discriminate.

Trauma is not something that happens to a select few. It is not something that only happens to those who are weak or vulnerable. It is a natural part of the human experience, something that we all have the potential to experience at some point in our lives.

The fact that trauma can happen to anyone is a reminder of the fragility of life. It is a humbling reminder that we are all human and can be thrown into a vulnerable position. But it can also be a reminder of our resilience and ability to overcome even the most difficult of challenges.

In the end, it is not about who is more or less susceptible to trauma. It is not about judging or categorizing people based on their experiences. It is about recognizing that trauma is a part of the human experience and that we all have the potential to overcome and recover from it. It is about coming together as a community to support each other through difficult times and create a more understanding, compassionate, and buoyant world.

We have tackled a myth about trauma. Now let's hammer in a few truths about trauma:

- It manifests in a variety of ways, such as anxiety, depression, chronic pain, and addiction.
- These experiences are often triggered by a range of harmful events, including abuse, neglect, and other forms of harm.

Facing trauma can be incredibly difficult and overwhelming. It requires us to confront our deepest fears, insecurities, and pain head-on. Often, we try to avoid or deny our trauma, pushing it deep down inside and pretending that it doesn't exist.

Unaddressed trauma can be likened to a dormant volcano – everything may appear calm on the surface, but a potential eruption is brewing just beneath. Just as a volcano can lie dormant for years, unresolved trauma can also remain buried within an individual for a long time, seemingly without consequence. However, the longer it goes unaddressed, the more likely it is to activate and manifest in ways that disrupt an individual's life.

When left unaddressed, trauma can silently seep into every aspect of a person's being, affecting their relationships, decision-making, and even their sense of self. It can feel as though a person is living a double life – one where everything appears normal to the outside world while another hidden reality takes place behind the scenes. It is a lonely and isolating experience, leaving individuals feeling as though they are the only ones going through this and that no one understands what they are experiencing.

Unaddressed trauma can also be like a chain reaction, where unresolved emotions and memories trigger other issues, leading to a snowball effect of mental and physical health problems. As with a pebble dropped in a pond, the ripples of trauma can spread far and wide, impacting not just the individual but their loved ones and their community.

Unaddressed trauma can be viewed as a missed opportunity for growth and transformation in the grand scheme of things. Attempting to overcome past instances is typically painful and challenging, but it can also be a catalyst for positive change. By facing and working through the trauma, individuals can develop greater resilience, empathy, and self-awareness. They can gain a deeper understanding of themselves and others and ultimately emerge stronger and more whole than before.

The human body is a remarkable vessel, capable of withstanding incredible physical and emotional stress. But even the strongest of us have our limits, and when we experience trauma, the body becomes a holding place for our pain and suffering. When we address that trauma, it can be removed from the body like an infected wound being lanced.

Furthermore, trauma can be passed down from generation to generation, impacting the lives of individuals and their families for years to come. Addressing trauma is, therefore, essential not only for the individual but also for the future of their family's well-being.

By addressing trauma, individuals can reclaim their lives from its effects. They can learn to cope with their symptoms and regain a sense of control over their lives, allowing them to move forward and achieve emotional and physical well-being.

One effective approach to addressing trauma is through understanding the role of sequencing in the body. Sequencing refers to the order and timing of movements, actions, and processes within the body. Trauma disrupts the natural sequencing of our physiological and psychological processes, leading to dysregulation of the mind and body.

However, there is hope. Developing self-awareness and understanding the sequencing of the body is essential for discharging trapped trauma and reestablishing a separation between the past and the present, so our bodies can tell the difference.

Why Self-Awareness Is So Important

Self-awareness is crucial for discharging trapped emotions because it allows individuals to recognize and understand their emotional and physical responses to trauma. Traumatic events can cause a range of emotional and physical reactions, such as anxiety, fear, numbness, hyperarousal, and dissociation. Without self-awareness, individuals may not even realize they are experiencing these reactions, or they may not understand why they are experiencing them.

By developing self-awareness, individuals can identify their emotional triggers and recognize when they are experiencing a traumatic response. This understanding can help them regulate their emotions and manage their responses to triggers, which can be an essential part of our journey to emotional well-being.

Self-awareness can also help individuals identify patterns in their thoughts, behaviors, and relationships that may be contributing to their trauma. Through self-reflection and self-exploration, individuals can gain insight into how past experiences have shaped their present-day experiences and develop strategies to cope with trauma.

Overall, self-awareness is crucial for discharging trauma because it allows individuals to take control of their journey, develop healthy coping strategies, and ultimately move forward in their lives.

But what does it really mean to be self-aware? While most of us have a general understanding of the term, the concept of self-awareness is actually made up of several layers. From recognizing our emotions and thoughts, understanding our values and beliefs, and becoming aware of how we show up in relationships, the journey to true self-awareness is a deep and transformative process. We'll now take a closer look at the layers of self-awareness and how they can help us better understand ourselves, the world around us, and the intricacies of our trauma.

Seven Layers of Self-Awareness

Acceptance

Trauma is a powerful force that makes it incredibly challenging to move beyond its impact. Many individuals try to avoid anything that reminds them of their trauma, but the trauma still lingers despite their efforts. Avoidance makes trauma more prominent in a person's thoughts, emotions, and behaviors. It's a tricky situation: The more you try to push it away, the more it becomes present in your life, affecting your ability to move on. This leads to feelings of helplessness and a sense that the trauma is in control rather than the survivor.

It's important to recognize that pain and suffering are not the same things. Our instinct is to avoid pain, whether it's physical or emotional, and we often try to push it away, numb it, or distract ourselves from it. However, in the case of trauma, avoidance leads to more suffering. When we judge and evaluate our pain, telling ourselves that it's bad, wrong, or unbearable, we amplify its impact on us. This judgment creates a mental and emotional struggle with the pain, making it harder to move through it and causing it to persist. This struggle can become all-consuming, leading to a sense of hopelessness and despair.

On the other hand, accepting the pain allows us to acknowledge and honor it as a part of our experience. By letting go of the judgment and struggle, we can move forward in a way that feels more authentic to ourselves.

Acceptance is a powerful tool in our somatic journey. It involves being open to internal experiences and willingly taking what is offered without protest or reaction. Acceptance does not mean that the experience of that trauma was okay, but rather it offers an alternative to the usual response to pain by reducing the struggle with it. By accepting the pain, you can move beyond it and find meaning.

In addition, acceptance suggests that you are more than your experience of trauma. You are a being who experienced, not a being who is the experience. This position of mindfulness and acceptance will help broaden your range of responses so that other meaningful outcomes can be pursued.

Mindfulness creates a place from which acceptance is possible, and by connecting with your sense of self, you move forward in the direction of your value. This is a crucial next step in acceptance, as it emphasizes taking action in the presence of painful and unwanted private experiences. Through the practice of mindfulness and acceptance, you can move beyond the trauma and find fulfillment and purpose in your life.

Take a moment to reflect on some of the challenging experiences from your past. By revisiting these experiences and acknowledging them for what they are, you begin to release the power they have over you. Don't try to rush the process! Take it slowly and approach it with an attitude of compassion and understanding. With time and patience, you can learn to accept and integrate these difficult elements of your past and move forward with greater resilience and self-awareness.

Writing them down helps to bring them into focus and makes them feel more tangible, so I encourage you to do this next exercise. Use your resources to regulate your experience if you find it emotionally difficult.

Accepting Your past

Create a list of the most challenging aspects of your past to repeatedly revisit them and gradually accept them.

Why am I having trouble accepting these experiences?

Segmenting

Have you ever felt like your emotions or experiences were just too much to handle? Trauma can leave us feeling overwhelmed and unable to process everything at once. That's where segmenting comes in. It's a psychological technique that helps break down these big, difficult feelings into smaller, more manageable parts.

The idea behind segmenting is separating the body and mind into different segments or parts rather than experiencing everything as one overwhelming whole. This makes it easier to process and deal with difficult experiences and emotions.

Trauma can leave our minds and bodies in a constant state of hyperarousal, which causes anxiety and feelings of being on edge. Segmenting highlights increased awareness of the different physical and emotional sensations we experience and gives us the tools to regulate our responses to them.

Beyond that, segmenting can also help us become more self-aware and understand ourselves better. By breaking down our experiences and emotions into smaller parts, we can identify patterns, triggers, and themes contributing to our mental health struggles.

Take a moment to tune in to your body and feel the separation of its parts. You can start with your legs, thighs, stomach, chest, head, or arms. Notice any sensations or things that you observe in each area. Practicing this regularly will allow you to feel your body as individual parts rather than as a single entity.

What do you notice about your body's parts?

As you begin to feel your body's individual parts, you may discover that certain areas hold different sensations or emotions. This awareness helps you better understand how your body responds to different situations and experiences. So, take your time, listen to your body, and explore the different parts it's made up of. With practice, you can learn to use this technique to gain deeper insight into yourself and your physical and emotional responses.

Identifying

It can be tough when a trigger reminds you of past trauma, and suddenly you're hit with intense emotional and behavioral reactions that make it feel like you're reliving that trauma all over again. You might have heard the term "triggered" used to describe emotional discomfort – so much so that it is commonplace – but for people who have experienced trauma, triggers can be terrifying, all-consuming, and often seemingly come out of nowhere.

A trigger can ignite a recollection of a traumatic event or a component of it. Triggers can show up in many different ways, such as a certain smell, sound, song, or even a piece of clothing. What triggers one person may not trigger another, as triggers are unique to each individual.

When you encounter a trigger, memories and thoughts associated with the trauma can come flooding back without warning. Intrusive thoughts are tough to control and lead to intense emotions and behavioral reactions. Triggers may make you feel helpless, panicked, unsafe, or overwhelmed with emotion.

The mind perceives triggers as a threat, which can prompt a response like fear, panic, or agitation. This reaction is a defense mechanism – the memory of the traumatic event places you right back into the experience, causing your walls to go up against the perceived threat to protect yourself.

While the severity of one's response to triggers will depend on the individual, it's normal to need some time for your nervous system to recover and return to a baseline state after encountering a trigger. Trauma can reduce your window of tolerance, which is the emotional zone in which you feel grounded, balanced, and calm. A smaller window of tolerance means that stressors are more likely to cause greater emotional upset.

Triggers are a defining feature of posttraumatic stress disorder (PTSD) and can serve as key events in which PTSD symptoms arise or are noticed. If you experience triggers, please know that seeking help from a mental health professional who can provide support and guidance can be incredibly beneficial in navigating the impact of trauma on your life. You don't have to face this alone.

Recovering from trauma can be a challenging and lengthy process. It may be tempting to avoid triggers or pretend they don't exist, but identifying your triggers and learning to manage them is the only true path to solace.

Whenever experiencing a trigger or a similar activation in any given setting, it is essential to remind yourself of where you are and that the traumatic event isn't actually happening. We must face our triggers head-on and dismantle them before they snowball. Learning to pause your flashbacks and bring yourself back to the present moment reminds your mind and body that the trauma is not currently happening, allowing you to self-regulate. This can take practice, but it will get easier over time, and your body will get better at dealing with it independently.

Self-Regulating When Experiencing Triggers

When you find yourself experiencing a flashback or trigger, check in with yourself to stay grounded in the present moment. Ask yourself the following questions in a gentle and non-judgmental way. Feel free to refer back to the describing words at the beginning of the book to give yourself a good baseline vocabulary.

How am I feeling right now? Are you frightened, anxious, distressed, sad, etc.?

What physical sensations am I noticing in my body? Are you trembling, sweating, or dizzy?

What memory or thought could be causing this reaction? This can include the bad person, the memory, or your childhood.

What is the current date and time?

Where am I right now?

What objects can I see around me? Name at least five things.

Because of my given scenario, I know the trauma isn't actually happening to me. Affirm this.

Triggers can come crashing in like a big wave and overwhelm you, making it hard to understand and cope with what's happening. However, taking the time to become aware of your triggers and learning to ride the wave instead of trying to fight against it is incredibly helpful in dealing with trauma. With practice, it will become easier to recognize and navigate your triggers instead of suppressing them or being controlled by them. This is an important step toward your emotional well-being.

Gaining the ability to identify the specific triggers that cause you to feel overwhelmed or distressed places you several steps closer to managing and overcoming them. For example, suppose you recognize that a certain sound or smell is triggering for you. In that case, you can take proactive measures to avoid or reduce your exposure to that trigger in the future until you can revisit it safely and release it from your being either with your therapist or with various exercises such as pendulation.

Furthermore, identifying the underlying reasons why certain triggers affect you will help you better understand your emotional and psychological reactions. This self-awareness allows you to develop coping strategies and build resilience over time. Many people use mindfulness techniques, deep breathing exercises, or resources to help them stay present and calm when they encounter a trigger.

One helpful technique for identifying triggers is carrying a notebook with you. Whenever you experience a trigger, jot down some notes about your thoughts, feelings, and the environment you were in. Through this, you will notice patterns and see connections between the different triggers you experience.

As you write down your observations, consider what you heard, saw, or smelled in that moment, as well as how you were feeling both physically and emotionally. This kind of sensory awareness can be particularly powerful in identifying triggers, as it helps you notice subtle environmental cues that might contribute to your reaction.

In addition to keeping a trigger log, you can also set aside some time each week to reflect on past triggers and try to remember what sensations were present when you experienced them. For example, you might recall a certain smell that triggered a flashback or a particular touch that made you feel anxious. By identifying these sensory triggers, you can build a more comprehensive understanding of what sets off your trauma responses, which can help you manage and confront them more effectively.

Working with a licensed psychotherapist should also be a consideration for helping you identify and work through your triggers. Ensure that this person (who is trained and experienced in trauma) understands the complexities of triggers and provides a safe and supportive environment for you. Professionals can provide you with a personalized treatment plan that considers your unique needs and circumstances.

Noticing

Noticing small changes in your emotions and body sensations is a powerful way to increase your self-awareness and emotional resilience. Pay attention to any slight shifts in your mood or physical sensations throughout the day. Tune in to them, and if you feel comfortable and safe, allow yourself to experience them fully instead of pushing them away. It could be a small feeling of tension, discomfort, anxiety, or even a memory of a past event. By learning to ride out these feelings instead of suppressing them, you prevent them from building up and becoming trapped within you. Trust yourself and allow yourself to feel. It's okay to be vulnerable and take the time to care for yourself this way.

Riding the Wave

Managing intense emotions in this way can be tough, but *Riding the Wave* is a practice that can help you surf through them. Imagine you're a surfer catching a powerful ocean wave; you don't fight it but instead move with it and ride its natural flow. In the same way, when dealing with strong emotions, learn to accept and ride them out instead of fighting them. Especially after practicing a somatic lifestyle for some time, your body will become better equipped to regulate itself.

Just like ocean waves, your emotions can be unpredictable and intense at times. Suppressing or acting out in harmful ways makes the situation worse and goes against your long-term goals and values. *Riding the Wave* encourages you to accept your emotions without judgment and experience them as they come and go, just like waves in the ocean.

Here are some tips to help you practice *Riding the Wave*:

- ❖ Be aware of the emotion: Name the emotion you're experiencing without judging yourself. Remember, the emotion is just something you're experiencing, not who you are.

- ❖ Experience it: Ride the wave of your emotions and accept them without trying to control them. It may be uncomfortable, but know that the feeling is temporary. Find a safe place and use your resources to calm yourself.

- ❖ Remember that the feeling is temporary and does not define you. You've been through difficult emotions before, and you can get through this one too.

- ❖ Receive and endure your emotions: Allow yourself to feel the emotion without assigning positive or negative thoughts to it. Accepting painful emotions without categorizing them frees you from suffering.

Riding the Wave does not take your trauma away, but it helps you make decisions from a wise mind. Acknowledging and accepting pain rather than trying to escape from it gives you clarity and focus.

Try this over the next week and write down your experiences and how they felt.

Talking To Your Past-Self

Talking to your past-self is an opportunity to give yourself the support you needed in the past but may not have received. It's natural to feel hesitant when you first hear about working with your past selves, but just as a firefighter enters a burning building to save those who are stuck, you are there to save your past selves, inadvertently freeing yourself from your past experiences.

When you go back to those difficult moments, you are not there to re-live the pain or let the emotions overwhelm you once again. You are there with a singular purpose – to save your past selves. It may be scary, but your past selves are waiting for you to provide the care and compassion they needed at the time.

So, let's get started on your mission to save your past selves. By doing this work, you can move forward with a greater understanding of your own needs. So, take a deep breath and trust that you have the strength and compassion to show up for yourself and your past selves by doing the following exercises:

Explore Which Part of You Needs Help

Our past selves play a significant role in shaping who we are today. When we feel anxious, afraid, angry, or confused, we need to analyze whether or not these emotions are rooted in one of our previous lives. That's why asking ourselves, "Who is feeling this way?" can be a helpful practice. Maybe it's a past version of yourself that experienced something difficult, like being verbally abused as a seven-year-old. Think of this practice as shining a light on the part of yourself that needs attention and care. When you do this, you can figure out who needs your help and give that part of yourself the support and attention it deserves so you can better understand and address the root of these emotions.

Write down your response when it comes to you, and remember that you have the power to overcome and support yourself through any challenge.

Who do you want to comfort? E.g., seven-year-old self.

Comfort your past self

Often, it's not you who is reliving the trauma, but a past version of yourself. So, approach yourself with a warm and gentle demeanor, as if you're talking to a younger version of yourself. You might ask questions like:

- What's going on for you right now?
- How are you feeling?
- How can you make your past self feel better?

Listen attentively to the answers that come up and record them below. Then, try to offer words of comfort and support that can help your past self feel seen, heard, and understood.

Ask your past self where they want to go

When you comfort your past self, ask them where they want to go, where they feel safe and happy. This is a beautiful opportunity to create a safe space for your past self to find comfort. Remember that you are not reliving the trauma – your past self is. You are there to provide them with the safety and comfort they need. It could be a favorite childhood spot, a beautiful park, or even a cozy corner in your imagination. Let your past self lead the way and follow them there with kindness and compassion. Describe this place below.

Release your past self

After taking your past self to a safe place and providing them with the comfort and joy they needed, you may notice a sense of relief and happiness within them. Take a moment to observe this beautiful transformation and feel proud of what you've provided for your past self. Allow yourself to bask in the warmth of this moment, knowing that you have taken a significant step towards physical and mental well-being.

Describe this feeling of transformation.

Write a Letter to Your Past Self

Write a letter to your past self, regardless of the length. Express anything you wish you had heard when you needed it the most, and address your past self as if you were a protective figure. I have added an extra page if you need more space or want to come back and do this again.

Dear,

Sincerely,

Just doing this exercise once won't magically fix everything, as personal growth takes time and consistency, but don't worry, it's a journey worth taking. If you find this exercise helps you, make it a regular part of your self-care routine. Over time, your subconscious mind will begin to understand that you're in a different place now and that your past self experienced the trauma, and its behind you. This realization is empowering and helps you move towards a more relaxed state of mind. Past events are often what triggers our fight or flight response, so practicing this exercise regularly helps train your nervous system to respond differently and differentiate between what has happened previously and what's happening now. So be patient with yourself, keep at it, and celebrate each small step forward.

Creating a Trauma Timeline to Find Patterns

One tool for exploring your trauma is creating a trauma timeline. Unique to every individual, a trauma timeline is a detailed history of one's painful life experiences that left them feeling abandoned, unsafe, confused, fearful, sad, angry, shameful, guilt-ridden, or stuck. A trauma timeline aims to:

1. Identify the distorted self-beliefs connected to these events.

2. Assess the methods for adapting, surviving, and avoiding the pain that accompanied the trauma.

3. Be able to differentiate past events from present, so we, and our bodies, can understand these events aren't happening anymore.

These distorted beliefs are often negative and self-critical. For example, someone who has experienced abuse may believe they are inherently unlovable or unworthy of affection. These beliefs can become deeply ingrained, affecting a person's self-esteem, relationships, and overall well-being.

Completing a trauma timeline will be a testing and vulnerable process, but the potential for creating a deeper connection with yourself and distinguishing between past and present will be advantageous. The timeline itself is a deeply explorative and powerful exercise. It helps victims find the courage to face their wounds, let go of beliefs that no longer serve them, and discover new empowering truths about themselves.

During the process of creating a trauma timeline, individuals may recall painful memories from their childhood or past experiences. Navigating and confronting these memories can be tricky. It is essential to create a safe and supportive environment for the process. Suppose you have a hard time reliving past events. In that case, it is important to do this with the supervision of a licensed therapist who will have useful techniques to facilitate the process and ensure your emotional well-being.

Approaching the creation of a trauma timeline can be done in different ways. The first way involves creating a timeline of events. This is especially helpful if your sense of time has become distorted. By creating a visual timeline, you better understand what you have been through and how it has affected you. It is okay if you don't remember everything at first – the timeline is a working document you can add to and edit over time.

Everyone with trauma experiences triggers, but not all triggers are immediately recognizable. Writing down or drawing your triggers alongside the timeline gains you a clearer understanding of what situations or stimuli cause you distress. Triggers can fall into the categories of taste, touch, smell, sight, and hearing, as well as feeling states. Explore each of these categories to help you anticipate and manage how trauma manifests in your life.

The great thing about these processes is that they create a bridge between your past and present, so your body can distinguish between the two. They are tangible, emboldening, and can be edited as you progress throughout your journey. Approach these activities with care.

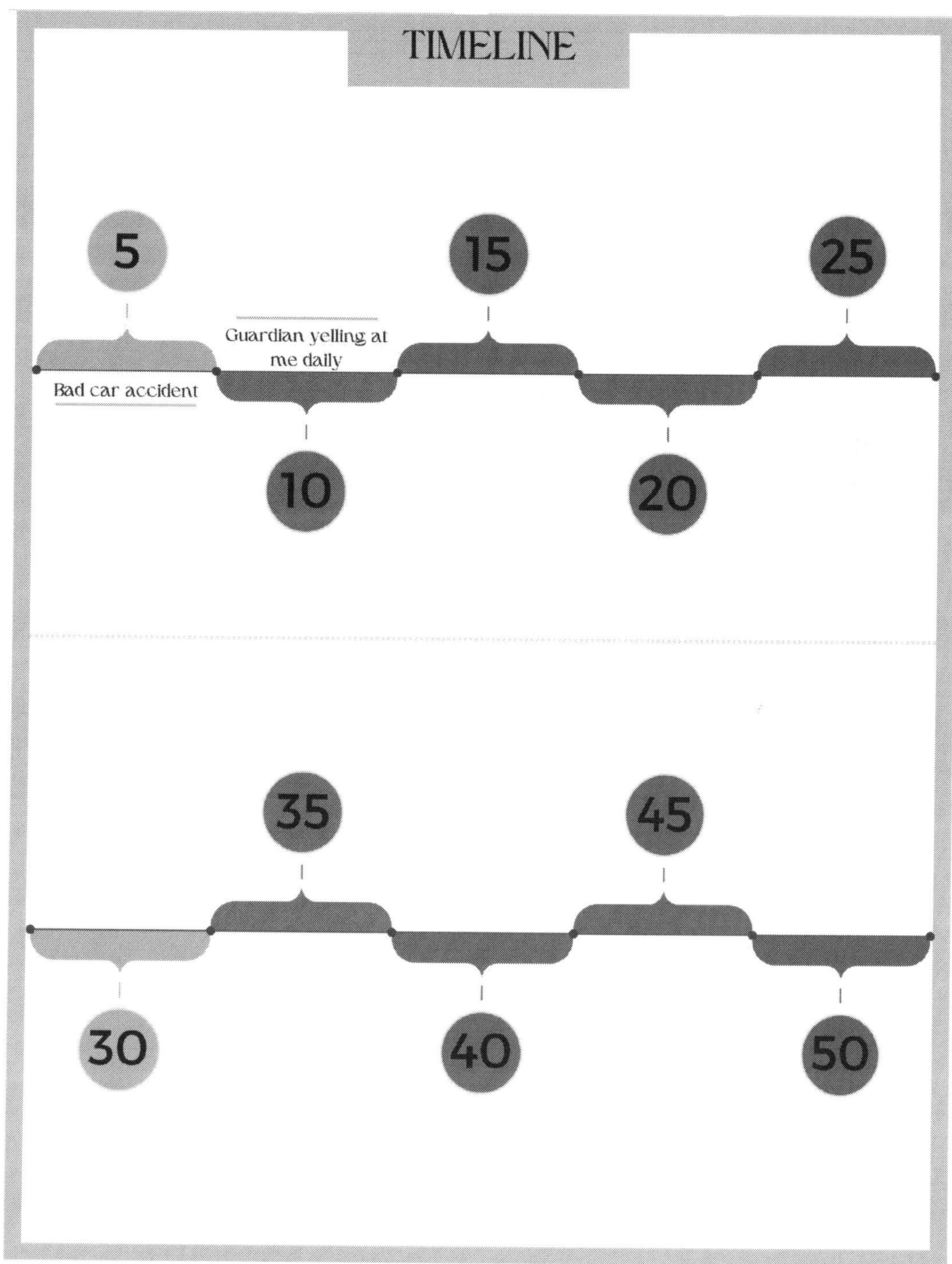
TIMELINE
5
15
25
Guardian yelling at me daily
Bad car accident
10
20
35
45
30
40
50

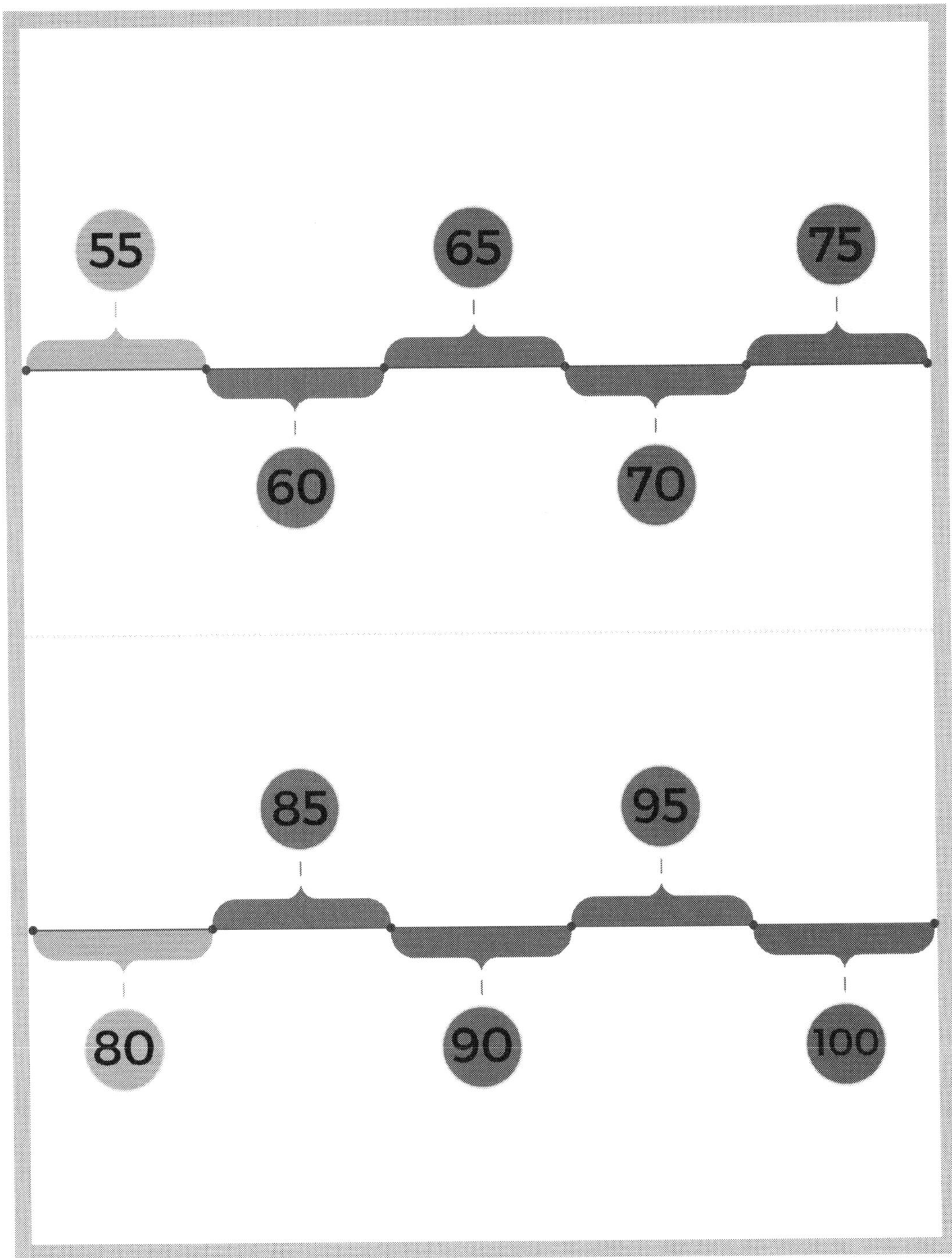
55
65
75
60
70
85
95
80
90
100

Do you notice any patterns in the timeline?

Note the most difficult period of your life. Go into as much detail as you would like.

Note the easiest or happiest period of your life. Go into as much detail as you would like.

Are there any negative experiences or timeframes that have led to positive outcomes?

Are there any time periods that are difficult for you to recall or seem hazy in your memory?

Are there any negative tenancies or beliefs that you've gained from past experiences that you still live out today?

Are these tendencies warranted, or are they false beliefs trapped from a complex time period?

The significance of creating a timeline is not to forget one's past or eliminate their engrained habits but to gain a deeper understanding of oneself without any sense of judgment. From there, you can move forward with a greater sense of self-awareness and empowerment, picking and choosing what you want to overcome.

Satisfaction Cycle

Have you ever stopped to consider how your early experiences shape your sense of self and the way you move through the world? According to Bonnie Bainbridge, the creator of Body Mind Centering, our developmental movement patterns play a significant role in our overall well-being and our ability to feel fulfilled in life.

At the heart of this idea is the satisfaction cycle. The premise is simple: When we are born, we begin to learn certain movement patterns that enable us to explore and interact with the world around us. As we master these movements and our ability to engage with our environment grows, we experience a sense of accomplishment and satisfaction.

For example, think about the feeling of reaching for something you want and being able to grab it with ease. It's a simple movement, but it can give you a powerful sense of competence and control over your surroundings. Similarly, being able to explore your environment with a sense of safety and security can help you develop a deep sense of self-assurance and confidence.

On the other hand, when we encounter obstacles or challenges that prevent us from mastering certain movements, we can experience frustration, anxiety, and a sense of inadequacy. This leads to a negative feedback loop where we become increasingly anxious or avoidant of new challenges, which only reinforces our negative self-image.

But let's not focus on the negative. Instead, I pose a question to you: Don't you think it is incredible that our exploration of the world begins before we are even born? Our natural reflexes, such as sucking, curling, reaching, and grasping, all play a vital role in helping us discover and understand ourselves.

Life's circumstances can disrupt this instinctual developmental process. Everyday events like the arrival of a new sibling or more significant events like trauma or neglect can alter our connection with our bodies. As we grow older, we tend to rely more on language and symbols, which further disconnects us from the simplicity of our embodied experience. And for those who have experienced trauma or neglect, movement impulses may have been overridden to survive.

This is where the satisfaction cycle comes in. When we know we can safely explore our environment, reach for what we want, and receive it, we experience a deep sense of accomplishment and gratification. Reconnecting with our instinctual selves rebuilds our sense of safety and agency in the world. It allows us to tap into the natural blueprints that guide our movements and brings us back to a place of embodied ease and confidence.

The good news is that it's never too late to work on these patterns and build a more positive relationship with your body and your environment. By paying attention to your movement patterns and exploring new ways of engaging with the world around you, you can begin to break out of old habits and develop a more positive feedback loop.

The satisfaction cycle is rooted in the innate movement patterns we learn during our earliest developmental stages. The cycle is made up of five basic movements, known as the "5 Basic Neurological Actions." They are:

- Yield
- Push
- Reach
- Grasp
- Pull

In our first year or two of life, these movements are relatively simple, such as pushing with our arms and legs or reaching with our hands and eyes. But as we grow and develop, these patterns become increasingly complex and involve more cross-lateral communication in the body, ultimately enabling us to crawl and eventually walk.

Return to these basic patterns and re-learn them with a sense of curiosity and openness by participating in this exercise:

Find a comfortable spot, preferably on the floor, where you can experience this intuitive movement sequence. Keep an open mind and approach this practice with curiosity, allowing your emotions to flow freely as they come. Trust your instincts.

Lie either on your back or belly and feel your body come into contact with the ground. ***Yield*** *to this contact by fully relaxing, taking a few deep breaths, and becoming aware of your connection with the floor.*

Look at the world as if you're seeing it for the first time. Is there anything that catches your eye or sparks your curiosity?

Next, ***Push*** *against the floor with your hands or forearms. Notice the engaged muscles and the strength you have.*

Allow your instincts to guide you to an object to interact with, and then ***Reach*** *for it. Once you've reached the object,* ***Grasp*** *it firmly and* ***Pull*** *it towards your chest. Pause and fully receive this moment, yielding back to the earth and experiencing the satisfaction of getting what you want.*

As you do this, keep bringing your awareness back to your body and the contact with the floor, feeling yourself push against the ground.

If any emotions arise, such as frustration, grief, or anger, take note of them and let them flow through you. Don't hold on to any tensions, and observe what may arise. Remember, it's natural to feel vulnerable in these moments.

By practicing these movements, you can reconnect with your instinctual self and experience the satisfaction cycle. Enjoy the process and trust your body's natural wisdom.

NOTES

Part 5:

Deepening Your Practice

"Yoga is the journey of the self, through the self, to the self."
- Bhagavad Gita

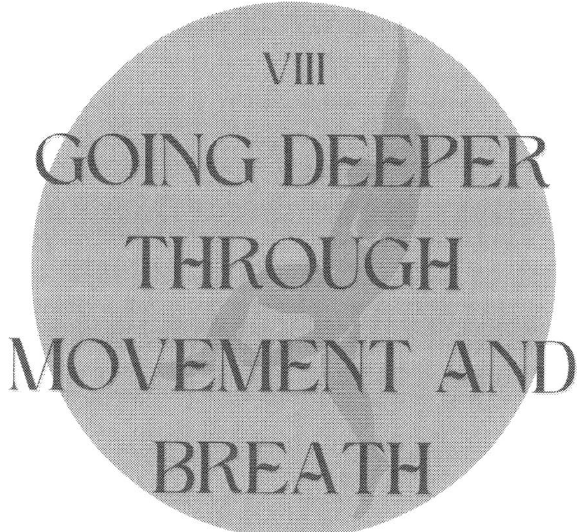

VIII GOING DEEPER THROUGH MOVEMENT AND BREATH

Breathing is crucial to our existence as living beings. We don't have to consciously think about it, but it happens continuously, about eighteen to twenty times per minute. That is over 25,000 times per day! This vital process brings oxygen into our bodies and releases carbon dioxide back into the air. But did you know that you can control your breathing with ease? By simply focusing on your breathing, you can regulate its pace, whether you want to slow it down or speed it up, or even pause for a moment.

The art of controlled breathing has been a part of spiritual practice for centuries. Spiritual leaders worldwide have used controlled breathing in meditation and prayer to achieve spiritual and physical well-being and to gain inner peace and clarity of mind. It's called breathwork, and it has been adapted by modern practitioners to help people in their daily lives. With breathwork, you can tap into the power of your breath to achieve a sense of calm, clarity, and relaxation.

What is Breathwork?

Breathwork is a tool used to promote physical, emotional, and spiritual well-being through the use of breath. Any practice involving intentional breathing is considered breathwork, and it can help people reduce stress and achieve personal growth. There are a variety of breathing patterns that people use to shape their breath consciously.

Deep breathing exercises are a common type of breathwork that practitioners use to help clients work through psychological pain, release physical tension, and promote a sense of calm. Breathwork can help individuals connect with their inner selves, fostering a greater sense of self-awareness and compassion.

One of the benefits of breathwork is that it can be done either with the guidance of a practitioner or on one's own. Self-directed techniques such as circular breathing and deep relaxation breathing can be practiced at home without the need for a professional. However, some schools of breathwork, such as Holotropic and Shamanic breathing, often require a facilitator to guide a more formal breathwork session.

No matter how it's practiced, breathwork has the potential to be a transformative experience, allowing individuals to connect with their breath and find a sense of inner peace and harmony.

The History of Breathwork

Breathwork techniques have a rich history dating back to ancient cultures in China, India, and Tibet. As early as 2700 B.C.E., Emperor Huang Ti of China supported the development of breathing exercises to promote mental and physical health. One of the most well-known practices that emerged from this era is qigong (also called energy cultivation), which includes over three thousand breathing methods. In India, breathwork was linked to the ancient practice of yoga, which has existed since 3000 B.C.E. Similarly, in Tibet, breathing exercises were developed to cultivate spirituality and help people cope with the region's climate.

Today, breathwork has become an important part of many modern therapies in psychology. Professionals in the field have developed numerous therapies incorporating breathwork to promote emotional well-being, reduce stress, and other numerous health benefits.

The benefits of breathwork are many, and the techniques used are diverse. Breathwork can be used to resolve psychological pain, release bodily tension, foster neutral emotion and soften psychological armor. But how does breathing, an act we take for granted all too often, grant us all these advantages? Let's answer that question next.

The Science of Breathwork

By consciously controlling one's breath, it is possible to affect both the sympathetic nervous system (SNS) and the parasympathetic nervous system (PNS), which have direct impacts on our body's responses to stress. Let's engage in a brief recall: The SNS is responsible for the body's fight or flight response, which is triggered by perceived danger, providing a burst of energy and adrenaline to prepare the body to respond. This response can contribute to health issues such as obesity, heart disease, and inflammation when it is activated chronically and unnecessarily. The SNS is responsible for a healthy immune system when activated properly in everyday life. Certain breathwork techniques can activate the SNS healthily, strengthening our immune system and building up our internal tolerance to stress. On the other hand, the PNS counteracts this response, bringing the body back to a state of relaxation.

Several studies have shown that slow, controlled breathing can activate the PNS, reducing heart rate and blood pressure and promoting relaxation. Breathwork techniques like deep breathing exercises can help practitioners learn to access this state of calm, even in stressful situations.

In 2018, a study conducted by Massachusetts General Hospital found that participants who underwent breathwork sessions that involved relaxation response training had a significant decrease in blood pressure, with many of them able to reduce or eliminate hypertension medication.

Moreover, hyperventilation through circular breathing is another method used in breathwork that stimulates the SNS. Although it might seem counterintuitive, mild hyperventilation has been shown to increase the levels of several substances that create energy in the body. This SNS stimulation can lead to increased focus and energy and a strong immune system.

Overall, breathwork offers a holistic approach to improving physical and emotional well-being. By understanding the impact of breathing on the body's nervous system, individuals can practice conscious breath control to reduce stress, promote relaxation, and increase focus and energy.

Three Relaxing Breathing Exercises

There are many breathwork techniques available, and it can be overwhelming to choose the right one. However, I have carefully selected a few contenders I believe are noteworthy for integrating into your daily routine. The three methods I have chosen stimulate the parasympathetic nervous system to initiate a relaxation response, which can be used in times of stress, during triggering exercises, or throughout your normal day to keep you in a state of calm.

Box Breathing

As mentioned in the body awareness chapter, box breathing is a popular form of yogic deep breathing technique that has been used by the United States Navy SEALs as well as individuals worldwide who find themselves feeling stressed or anxious. Don't be surprised if you hear it referred to by other names such as four-by-four breathing, 4-4-4-4 breathing, equal breathing, or square breathing.

The name "box breathing" is derived from the concept of a four-sided box. This concept is reflected in the breathing pattern of slowly counting to four for a total of four times, including four counts of inhaling, holding the breath, exhaling, and holding again after the exhale.

Box breathing, like other forms of breathwork, can have a significant impact on the body and can provide a variety of benefits. One of the most notable benefits of box breathing is its ability to reduce stress and promote relaxation. Other benefits include:

- Effective at activating the parasympathetic nervous system, the bodily system responsible for rest and digestion.

- Aids in calming the mind even during times when individuals are not experiencing stress or anxiety, as it can be seamlessly incorporated into daily life as mindfulness.

While box breathing is a simple technique, it can take some time to master. Remember not to rush yourself as you go through the steps, as you want to maintain a comfortable pace.

Here are the steps for practicing box breathing:

1. Gently release all the air from your lungs as you exhale slowly.

2. Inhale through your nostrils and slowly count to four in your mind. Take note of the feeling of the air flowing into your lungs and filling your abdomen.

3. Hold your breath for a count of four.

4. Release another slow exhale over a count of four.

5. Hold your breath for another count of four.

6. Complete three to four cycles of this breathing pattern.

This is a straightforward breathwork exercise and is a great place to start. Try doing it once or twice a day. I like doing it in the morning to prepare for the day and at night to wind down and sleep better. Keep practicing, and it will become easier to calm yourself during times of stress or anxiety.

Deep Relaxation Breathing

Deep relaxation breathing (DRB) is also known as diaphragmatic breathing, relaxation breathing, or abdominal breathing. It is commonly used in various fields, such as nursing, dentistry, and public health. It is a self-practice that can be performed without a facilitator.

This technique involves taking deep breaths, expanding the diaphragm, and exhaling slowly. This practice activates the parasympathetic nervous system (PNS) and reduces the activity of the sympathetic nervous system (SNS). Studies suggest that this specific breathing pattern can lower blood pressure, decrease heart rate, and help manage symptoms of anxiety, aggression, and posttraumatic stress disorder (PTSD).

This technique is usually practiced with closed eyes to achieve deep relaxation through breathing, and it involves taking deep inhalations, expanding the diaphragm, and slowly exhaling. Here are the steps to follow:

1. Breathe in for four counts.

2. Hold your breath for seven counts

3. Breathe out for eight counts.

Do this continually; try for anywhere from five to thirty minutes.

Breathe Like a Monk

Breathing is an essential function of the human body. It sustains our life force and keeps us going. For monks, however, breathing is much more than just a bodily function. It is a way of life, a path to enlightenment, and a means of connecting with the universe.

To a monk, breathing is a reminder of the constant ebb and flow of life, the cyclical nature of the universe. With every breath, they inhale the energy of the universe, and with every exhale, they release their worries and fears.

Breathing is also a means of purifying the mind and body. Through deep, intentional breathing, monks can release the negative energy that has accumulated within them, cleansing their minds and bodies of impurities. This allows them to achieve a state of heightened awareness, a state of pure consciousness in which they are more attuned to the universe and their place within it.

But perhaps most importantly, breathing is a way of attaining inner peace. In a world full of chaos and uncertainty, breathing offers a moment of respite, a moment of stillness in which one can connect with the universe and find balance. By focusing on their breath, monks can quiet the constant chatter of the mind, silencing the doubts and fears that so often plague us in our daily lives.

If you don't want to follow a structured breathing exercise or count your breaths, try breathing slowly through your nose into your belly or 'energy center' below the naval, like a monk would. Focus on the buzzing energy around your head, which will gradually dissipate and fall to your belly with each breath. Pay attention to every breath and be present in the current moment. It's a simple but effective way to calm yourself. This technique is called diaphragmatic breathing. It involves breathing deeply from the belly rather than shallowly from the chest. This technique is believed to calm the mind and reduce stress, as it stimulates the vagus nerve, which helps regulate the body's relaxation response. Focusing on your breath throughout everyday life is a great way to keep your baseline and stay present.

If and when these exercises become easy and sufficient for you, you can expand into the diverse world of breathwork. There are many techniques and methods of controlled breathing and hyperventilation to create all sorts of bodily sensations and a wide array of health benefits. The scope is kept small in this book because our primary goal is to introduce calm into your life.

Somatic Yoga

Somatic yoga is a type of yoga practice that focuses on the awareness of internal physical sensations, movement patterns, and breath. It can be beneficial for people who are looking to improve their physical health and mobility, reduce stress and anxiety, and enhance their mind-body connection. Somatic yoga helps to release tension and tightness in the body, improve posture and balance, and increase flexibility and range of motion. It can also be used as a form of meditation, allowing practitioners to become more present in the moment and cultivate a sense of inner calm and relaxation. Overall, somatic yoga offers a holistic approach to wellness that supports both physical and mental well-being.

My Six Favorite Somatic Yoga Poses

Easy Pose (Sukhasana)

A humble and grateful place. Although it seems simple, it can actually be quite challenging. When done correctly, you will feel calm and relaxed, and your body will create a foundation to manage stress. A great way to deactivate our fight-or-flight response and initiate relaxation.

Legs Up the Wall Pose (Viparita Karani)

This is an excellent pose to bring relief to your lower back, ease anxiety and restore the body and mind. You can stay in this longer than specified if you desire.

Tree Pose (Vrikasana)

A great way to focus the mind on a single point called the "dristi point," which can tame a busy mind. This pose removes you from thoughts of anxiety and stress and requires a calm mind, smooth breath and steady focus.

Cat-cow Pose (Chakravakasana)

Cat-cow pose can increase the flexibility of the shoulders, neck, and spine. The movement also stretches the muscles of the hips, back, abdomen and chest releasing tension throughout the body.

Childs Pose (Balasana)

A great pose to fully relax. It releases tension in the back, neck and shoulders. It can also relieve anxiety, open our hips and back and increase blood flow, restoring ourselves. The integration with a steady and elongated breath creates a calm and relaxing "rest and restore response" in our bodies.

Crocodile Pose (Makarasana)

The Crocodile pose facilitates diaphragmatic breathing which correlates with the harmonious functioning of the nervous system by triggering the relaxation response. The abdomen rests on the floor, expanding the lower back and ribs, reducing tension in the shoulders and spine and calming anxiety.

To access the complete routine and instructions for each pose, download it from BecomingTheSoma.com or scan the QR code below with your cell phone camera.

Somatic Stretching

A crucial component of maintaining physical health and well-being is stretching. It can aid in easing muscle tension, preventing injuries, and enhancing your posture, flexibility, and range of motion. Traditional stretching methods, however, frequently ignore the interaction between the body, mind, and emotions in favor of concentrating just on the physical mechanics of the movement. This is where somatic stretching comes in.

Somatic stretching is a holistic method emphasizing conscious body awareness and the relationship between the mind and body. Somatic stretching supports gentle, mindful motions that activate the body's inherent intelligence and awareness, as opposed to other stretching methods that focus on forceful movements or passive holds. We can relax and become more flexible in a way that feels secure, sustainable, and advantageous for our general well-being by listening to our internal feelings and following the body's cues.

Its benefits extend beyond physical health, including emotional regulation, stress reduction, and a more profound sense of embodiment and self-awareness.

Here are my five favorite somatic stretches. Do them whenever you have the time and want to ground yourself, individually or sequentially.

Pelvic Tilt: While lying on your back with your knees bent and feet flat, Inhale, then exhale and gently arch your back toward the sky. After that, flatten your lower back against the ground and tilt your pelvis toward your belly button. Hold for a few seconds, release and repeat the sequence.

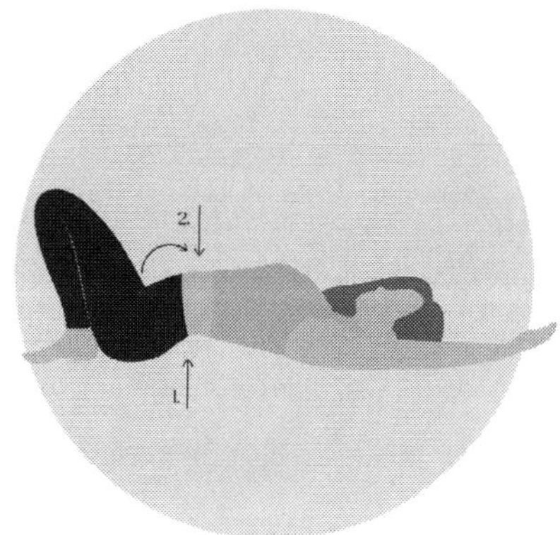

Spinal Twist: While lying on your back with your knees bent and feet flat, extend your arms out to the sides with your palms facing down. Inhale, exhale and drop both knees to one side, twisting your spine. Hold for a few seconds, then repeat on the other side. Trust your body and don't go further than youre comfortable.

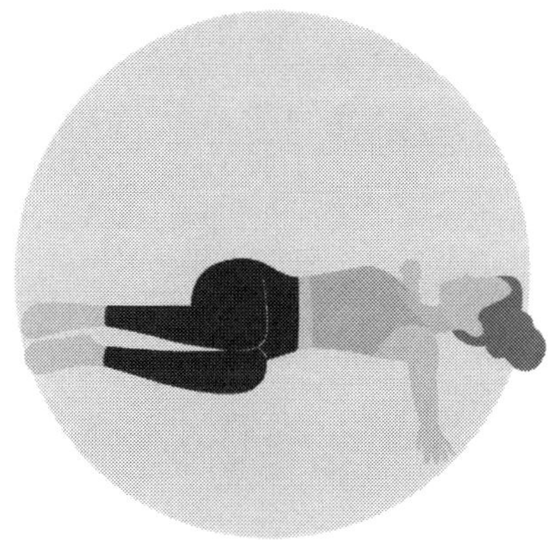

Neck Release: Start by sitting comfortably and taking a few deep breaths. Slowly tuck your chin towards your chest, allowing the back of your neck to stretch gently. Next, relax your neck and tilt your head to one side, bringing your ear towards your shoulder without pushing or straining. Breathe deeply and relax into the stretch. You can pull your head slightly to aid in the stretch as you progress. Then, tilt your head to the opposite side and repeat the process. Finally, repeat the sequence from the beginning, slowly and mindfully, with each stretch. Do this 3-5 times or whatever feels comfortable for you.

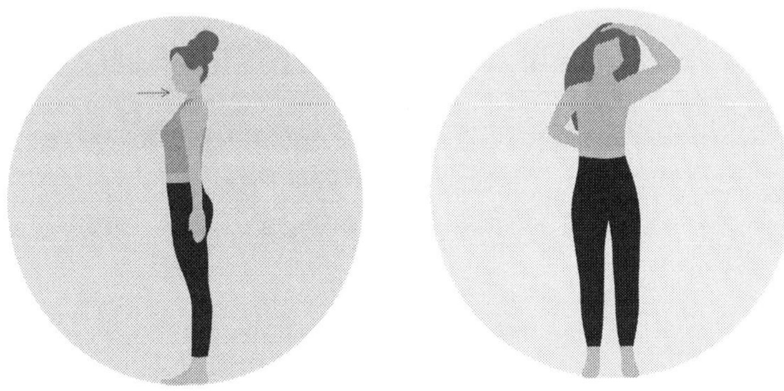

Side Bend Stretch: Stand with your arms by your sides and your feet hip-width apart. Take a breath, then let it out as you extend your right arm above your head and slant your body to the left. Maintain your hips level and your feet firmly on the ground. Repeat on the opposite side after holding for a short while. Repeat as desired.

Figure Four Stretch: While lying on your back with your knees bent and feet flat, Cross your left ankle over your right knee and gently pull your right knee towards your chest. Hold for a few seconds, then release and repeat on the other side.

Utilizing somatic stretching and yoga in everyday life is a powerful method that promotes mind-body integration through conscious movement and body awareness. Somatic movement can help us feel more grounded, embodied, and self-aware, leading to improved physical health and greater emotional and physical well-being.

NOTES

CONCLUSION

Trauma is an inevitable part of life, regardless of its weight or impact. It affects everyone. We all carry a lifetime of unique experiences, memories, and emotions that shape our identity and interactions with the world. These experiences can feel like a heavy burden, causing both physical and emotional pain, which can limit our beliefs and behaviors and leave us with a sense of lacking in our lives. The weight of these experiences can be so severe that it may seem impossible to shake off their hold on us.

However, this book presents a revolutionary concept. What if we could access the wisdom of our bodies to not only comprehend but also alleviate these traumas? What if we could release the constraints of the past and consciously and intentionally delve into our minds to embark on a brighter and more fulfilling future?

This concept becomes a reality through somatic therapy. This holistic approach recognizes the deep interconnections between the mind and body, utilizing this understanding to facilitate restoration and personal growth. Somatic therapy is becoming increasingly popular because it works, and you do not have to stand by and miss out on the benefits that many others are already experiencing by consistently utilizing the techniques encouraged by this approach to health and wellness.

This book serves as an invitation to embark on a journey toward emotional well-being, transformation, and personal growth, ultimately unlocking the true potential of your mind and body.

A significant portion of society operates as though the mind and body are separate entities, a belief that has been deeply ingrained in Western culture for some time. However, they are both integral components of our being. A lack of unity between the two results in intense suffering. Millions of people are paying the price for this belief, as it manifests in a variety of ways, such as physical pain, anxiety, depression, and stress. It can feel as if we are in a constant state of fight or flight, detached from the present and unable to find inner peace. There is a persistent undercurrent of discomfort, an ongoing feeling of being not quite right.

When the mind and body are not in harmony, it becomes challenging to navigate the world around us, resulting in difficulties in building and maintaining relationships, as well as distress in pursuing our passions and dreams. Life can feel meaningless, and purpose can seem elusive. Have you ever felt lost and disillusioned? Have you ever experienced isolation, feeling alone even when surrounded by loved ones?

The good news is that you don't have to feel this way. By accessing the wisdom of your body, you can understand past traumas, ultimately unlocking the true potential of your mind to live a happy, fulfilled, and healthy life. Somatic therapy offers this possibility.

However, achieving success with somatic therapy is not a quick fix or a one-size-fits-all solution. Like any other form of therapy, it requires consistency in doing exercises and changing thought patterns that have held you back in the past. It takes time to see change occur. Think of yourself as a butterfly within a cocoon, allowing nature to take its course to emerge beautifully transformed. You may make mistakes or may need to work through several methods before finding those that are most effective. You may even fall off the bandwagon with the exercises. But allow yourself grace and patience as you put in the work. Be committed to gaining results despite the obstacles you face, persisting even as you confront uncomfortable emotions and memories.

When starting your journey of somatic therapy, it's crucial to have clear goals in mind. What does personal growth mean to you? Having a general sense of direction, even if it changes over time, helps you measure your progress and fuel your motivation to keep going.

It's also essential to be open to the process because emotional progression isn't always linear, especially as you uncover aspects of yourself you didn't know existed. The initial actions you take may work, but as more of your past surfaces, you may need to make adjustments. Keeping an open mind and trusting the process, even if it's not what you expected, is critical to your success.

Although somatic therapy requires tremendous effort, you don't have to do it alone. This book can be a helpful companion throughout your journey. Embrace the practice as part of your lifestyle for a seamless transition into a new way of thinking and living.

In addition to the exercises and techniques presented in this book, it's important to have a support system in place. This may include a therapist, support group, or trusted friend or family member who can provide emotional support and encouragement as you work through the process of somatic therapy.

Good luck as you continue forward on your courageous journey. Reuse this book as much as you like and remember to use any exercises you find useful as a daily or weekly habit.

Studies

I have mentioned various studies throughout the book, and I've listed them below if you'd like to do further research on specific topics.

Specific Transcriptome Changes Associated with Blood Pressure Reduction in Hypertensive Patients After Relaxation Response Training

https://www.liebertpub.com/doi/10.1089/acm.2017.0053

Somatic Experiencing for Posttraumatic Stress Disorder: A Randomized Controlled Outcome Study.

https://www.ncbi.nlm.nih.gov/pmc/articles/PMC5518443/

The effects of chronic stress on health: new insights into the molecular mechanisms of brain-body communication.

https://www.ncbi.nlm.nih.gov/pmc/articles/PMC5137920/

An Exploratory Study of a 3-Minute Mindfulness Intervention on Compassion Fatigue in Nurses.

https://pubmed.ncbi.nlm.nih.gov/33953010/

Brief, daily meditation enhances attention, memory, mood, and emotional regulation in non-experienced meditators.

https://www.sciencedirect.com/science/article/abs/pii/S016643281830322X

How Breath-Control Can Change Your Life: A Systematic Review on Psycho-Physiological Correlates of Slow Breathing

https://www.ncbi.nlm.nih.gov/pmc/articles/PMC6137615/

References

2020 presidential election a source of significant stress for more Americans than 2016 presidential race. (2020, October 7). https://www.apa.org. https://www.apa.org/news/press/releases/2020/10/election-stress

Chronic stress, cortisol dysfunction, and pain: A Psychoneuroendocrine rationale for stress management in pain rehabilitation. (n.d.). PubMed Central (PMC). https://www.ncbi.nlm.nih.gov/pmc/articles/PMC4263906/

Depression. (2021, September 13). World Health Organization (WHO). https://www.who.int/news-room/fact-sheets/detail/depression

Gillette, H. (n.d.). *EMDR therapy: How it works, benefits, uses, and side effects*. Psych Central. https://psychcentral.com/health/emdr-therapy

"Brain over body"–A study on the willful regulation of autonomic function during cold exposure (n.d.). Just a moment... https://www.sciencedirect.com/science/article/abs/pii/S1053811918300673?via%3Dihub

PMC site is overloaded. (n.d.). National Center for Biotechnology Information. https://www.ncbi.nlm.nih.gov/pmc/articles/PMC3951033/

Self-efficacy and the perception of control in stress reduction. (2019, March 13). MentalHelp.net. https://www.mentalhelp.net/stress/self-efficacy-and-the-perception-of-control-in-stress-reduction/

Somatic experiencing for posttraumatic stress disorder: A randomized controlled outcome study. (n.d.). PubMed Central (PMC). https://www.ncbi.nlm.nih.gov/pmc/articles/PMC5518443/

Stress Management Versus Lifestyle Modification on Systolic Hypertension and Medication Elimination: A Randomized Trial (n.d.) Mary Ann Liebert, Inc. https://www.liebertpub.com/doi/10.1089/acm.2007.0623

Traumatic stress: Effects on the brain. (n.d.). PubMed Central (PMC). https://www.ncbi.nlm.nih.gov/pmc/articles/PMC3181836/ *Voluntary hypocapnic hyperventilation lasting 5 MIN and 20 MIN similarly reduce aerobic metabolism without affecting power outputs during Wingate anaerobic test*. (n.d.). PubMed.

Greenwald, A. (2021, February 11). *4 Tips to Easily Ride through a Wave of Emotions*. Empower Your Mind Therapy. Retrieved March 3, 2023, from https://eymtherapy.com/blog/tips-ride-wave-of-emotions/

Consultants, P. (2020, October 20). *Acceptance in the Treatment of Trauma*. Brisbane Psychologists. Retrieved March 3, 2023, from https://psychologyconsultants.com.au/acceptance-in-the-treatment-of-trauma/

Hoshaw, C. (2021, February 26). *Body Awareness: How to Deepen Your Connection with Your Body*. Healthline. Retrieved March 3, 2023, from https://www.healthline.com/health/mind-body/body-awareness

K. (2022, December 27). *How Box Breathing Can Help You Destress*. Cleveland Clinic. Retrieved March 3, 2023, from https://health.clevelandclinic.org/box-breathing-benefits/

THC Editorial Team. (2022, January 26). *Breathwork: Science, Types, and Benefits of Breathing Exercises*. The Human Condition. Retrieved March 3, 2023, from https://thehumancondition.com/breathwork-science-types-benefits/

Center, C. B. Y. A. (2021, March 23). *Experiential Exploration of Trauma via Timeline*. Claudia Black Center. Retrieved March 3, 2023, from https://www.claudiablackcenter.com/experiential-exploration-of-trauma-via-timeline/

Permanente, K. (n.d.). *Forest bathing: What it is and why you should try it*. Retrieved March 3, 2023, from https://healthy.kaiserpermanente.org/health-wellness/healtharticle.what-is-forest-bathing

Schenck, L. (2017, March 6). Increase Somatic Awareness with a Body Scan Mindfulness Exercise. Mindfulness Muse. Retrieved March 3, 2023, from https://www.mindfulnessmuse.com/mindfulness-exercises/increase-somatic-awareness-with-a-body-scan-mindfulness-exercise

Smith, K. & Rothchild, B. (2009). *Mindfulness: Appendix E: Flashback protocol*. Living Well. Retrieved March 3, 2023, from https://learn.livingwell.org.au/mod/page/view.php?id=138

Hahn, L. (2023, February 6). Orlando Therapist: Tools for Anxiety - Somatic Resources. Mindful Living Counseling Orlando.Retrieved March 3, 2023, from https://www.mindfullivingcounselingservices.com/blog/2019/7/8/tools-for-anxiety-somatic-resources

R. (2020, January 14). Somatic Experiencing: A Body-Centered Approach to Treating PTSD. Lyn-Lake Psychotherapy & Wellness. Retrieved March 3, 2023, from https://therapy-mn.com/blog/somatic-experiencing-ptsd/

Wikipedia contributors. (2022, December 4). Somatic psychology. Wikipedia. Retrieved March 3, 2023, from https://en.wikipedia.org/wiki/Somatic_psychology

Schwartz, A. (2018, July 31). Somatic Psychology and the Satisfaction Cycle | Dr. Arielle Schwartz. Arielle Schwartz, PhD. Retrieved March 3, 2023, from https://drarielleschwartz.com/somatic-psychology-satisfaction-cycle-dr-arielle-schwartz/

I. (2022a, August 19). Somatic psychotherapy tools: resourcing, titration and pendulation. InnerCamp. Retrieved March 3, 2023, from https://innercamp.com/somatic-psychotherapy-tools-resourcing-titration-and-pendulation/

Lebow, H. I. (2021, June 3). Can You Recover from Trauma? 5 Therapy Options. Psych Central. March 3, 2023, from https://psychcentral.com/health/trauma-therapy

Pedersen, T. (2021, August 18). All About Somatic Therapy. Psych Central. March 3, 2023, from https://psychcentral.com/blog/how-somatic-therapy-can-help-patients-suffering-from-psychological-trauma

What Everyone Should Know About Past Self Work. (2020, April 12). Katie Maloney Coachi. March 3, 2023, from https://www.katiemaloneycoaching.com/post/what-everyone-should-know-about-past-self-work

Made in the USA
Middletown, DE
16 August 2024